BENEFITS OF COLORING IN MANDALAS

Coloring in mandalas can offer a variety of benefits for mental, emotional, and even physical well-being. Here are 10 potential benefits:

Stress Reduction: Coloring mandalas can be a meditative and calming activity that helps reduce stress and anxiety levels by promoting relaxation and focus on the present moment.

Mindfulness Practice: Engaging in coloring requires focus and attention, making it a form of mindfulness practice that can help you stay grounded and fully present.

Creativity Enhancement: While coloring within the lines of a mandala design, you can experiment with color combinations, shading, and patterns, stimulating your creative thinking.

Emotional Expression: Coloring can serve as a non-verbal way to express emotions and feelings, providing an outlet for processing and releasing pent-up emotions.

Fine Motor Skills: The intricate nature of mandala designs encourages fine motor skill development, which can be especially beneficial for children but also for adults as a form of cognitive exercise.

Focus and Concentration: Coloring within the detailed patterns of a mandala requires sustained focus and concentration, which can improve your ability to concentrate on tasks in other areas of life as well.

Color Psychology: The choice of colors can influence mood and emotions. Engaging with mandalas allows you to experiment with different color combinations that reflect your current emotional state or help you achieve a desired mood.

Self-Expression: Mandala coloring provides an opportunity for self-expression through color choices and design preferences, allowing you to connect with your inner self in a unique way.

Sense of Accomplishment: Completing a mandala coloring session can give you a sense of achievement and satisfaction, boosting self-esteem and confidence.

Cognitive Relaxation: Engaging in an activity like coloring can provide a break from overthinking or ruminating, giving your cognitive processes a chance to rest and recharge.

Remember that individual experiences may vary, and while many people find these benefits from coloring mandalas, others might have different reactions. Ultimately, the key is to engage in activities that bring you joy, relaxation, and a sense of well-being.

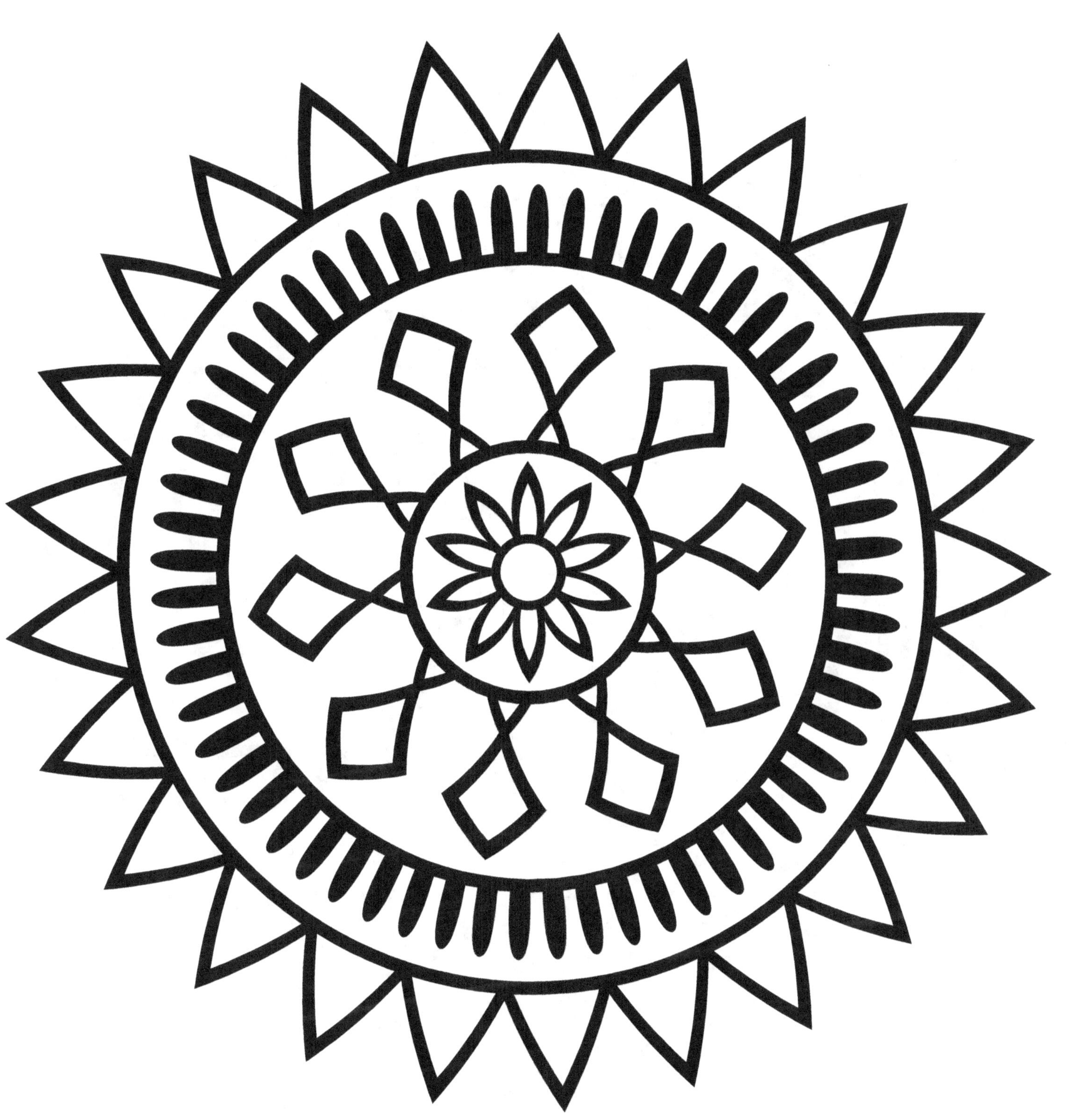

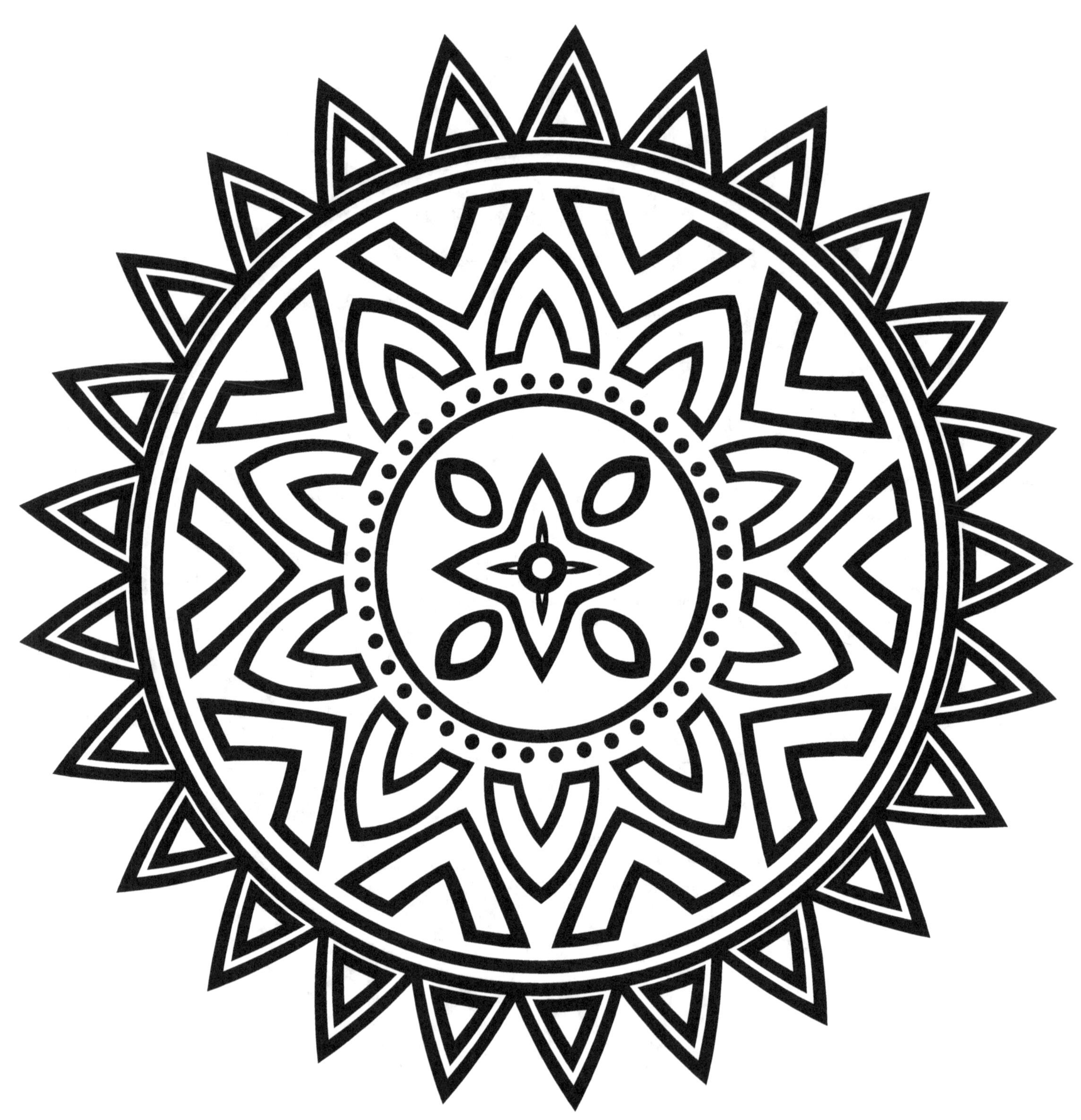

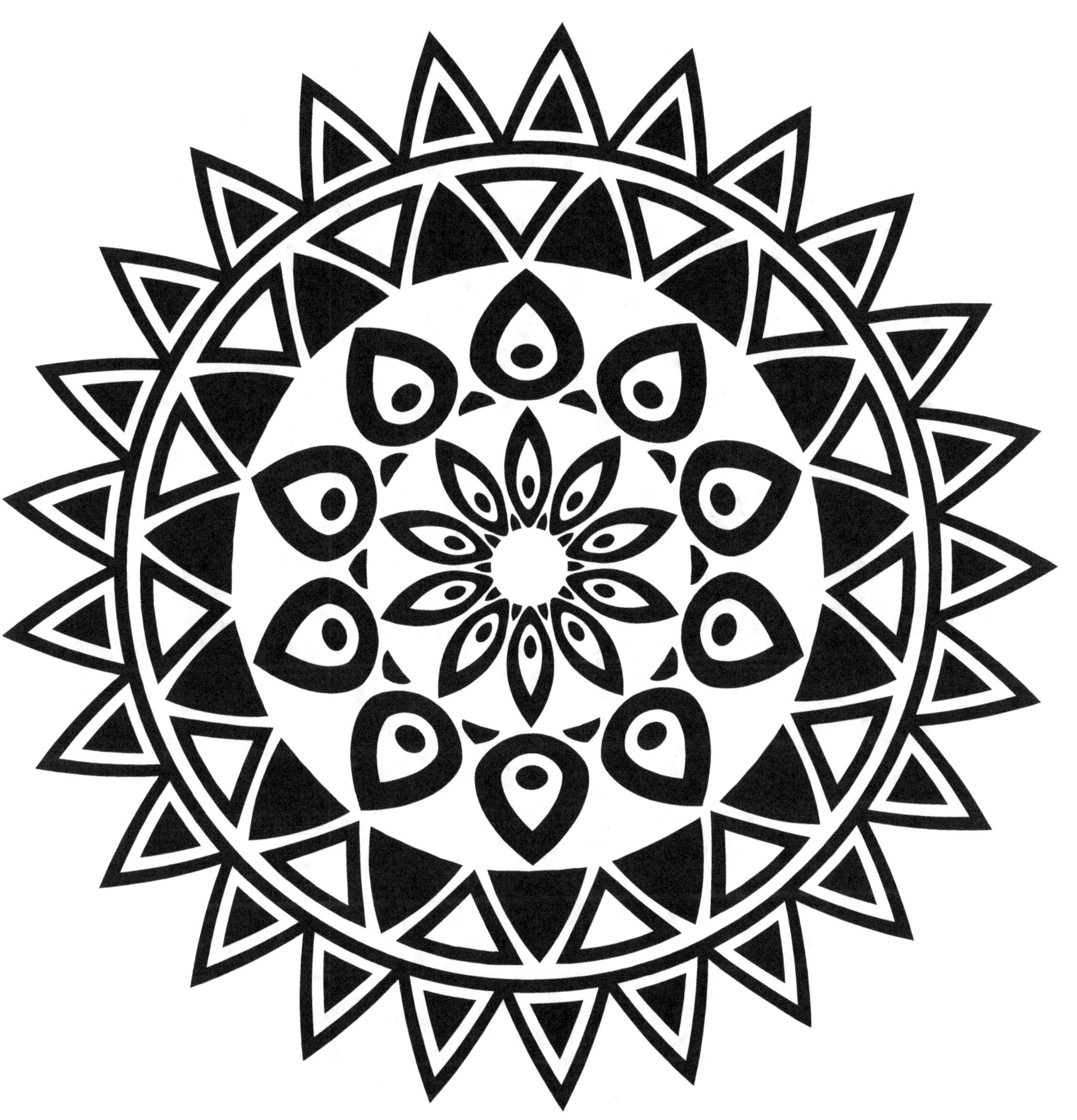

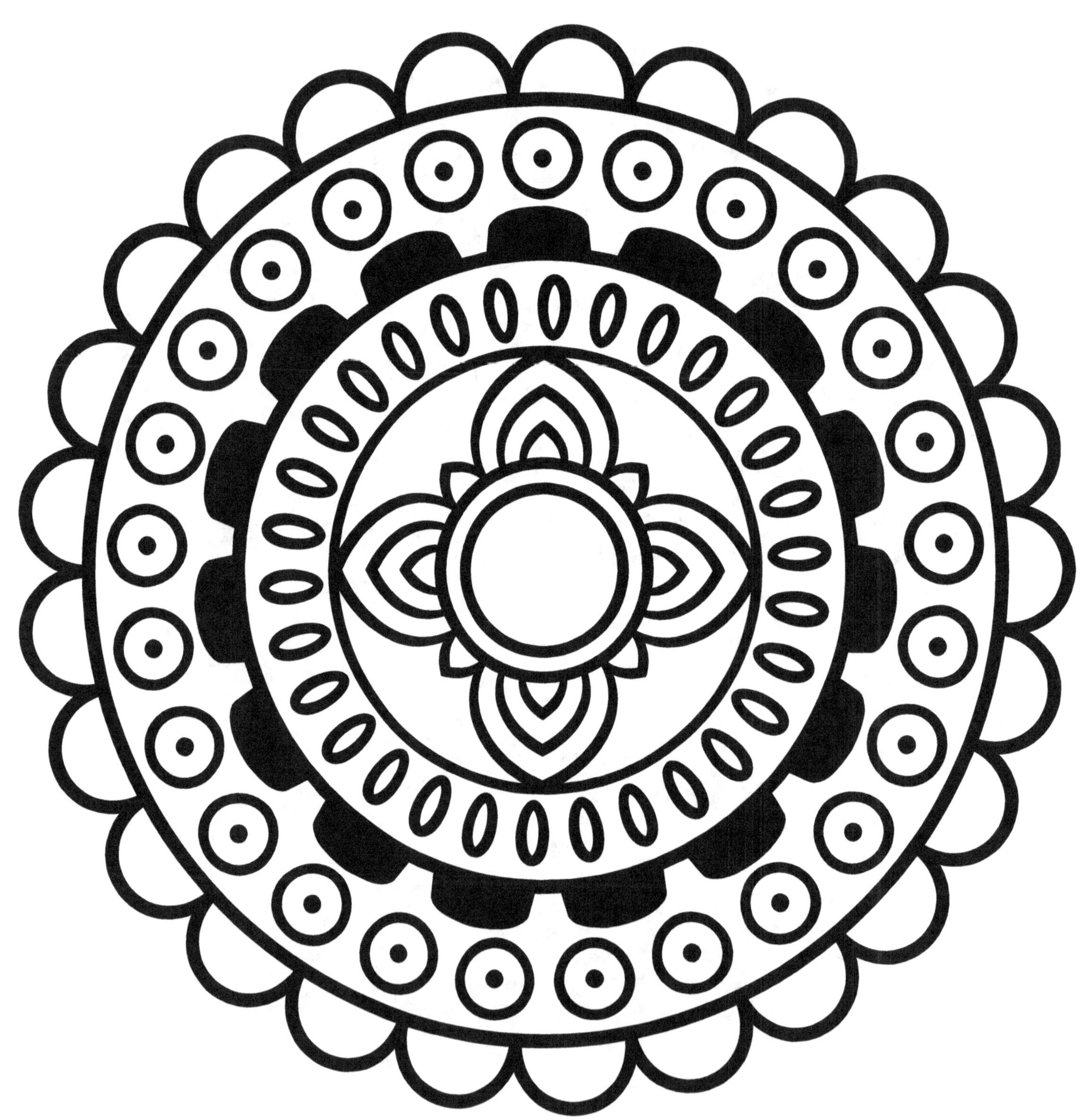

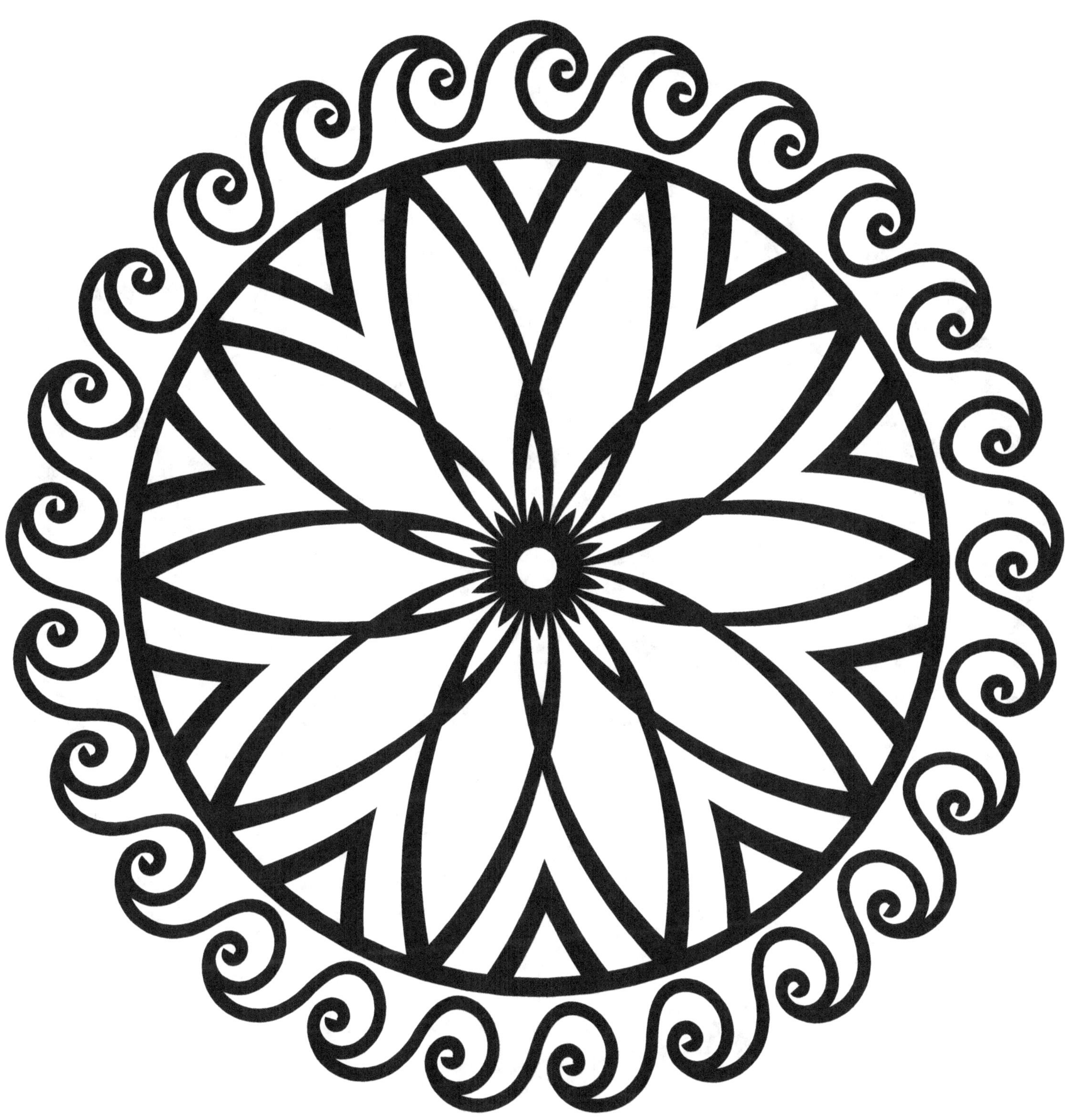

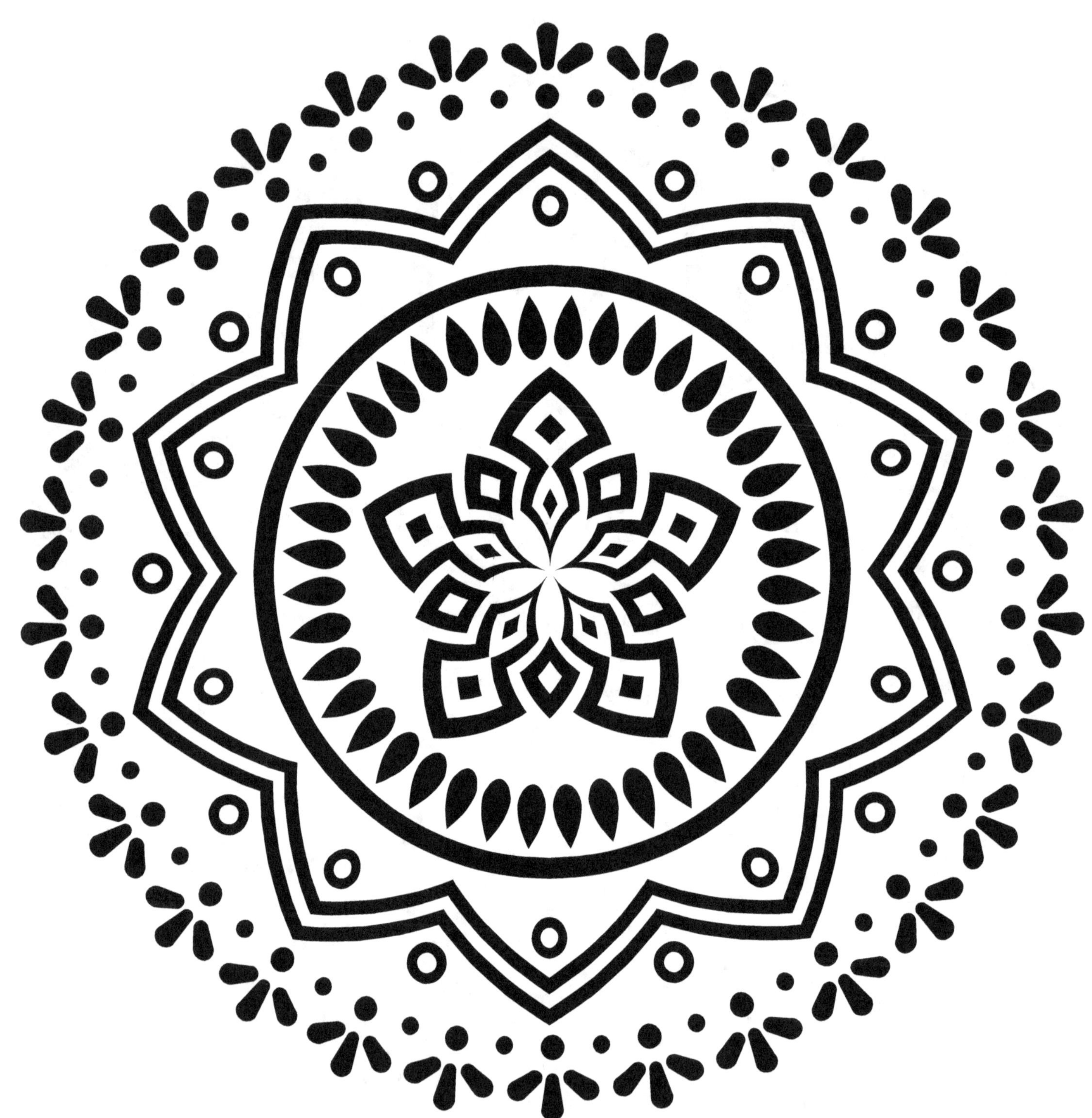

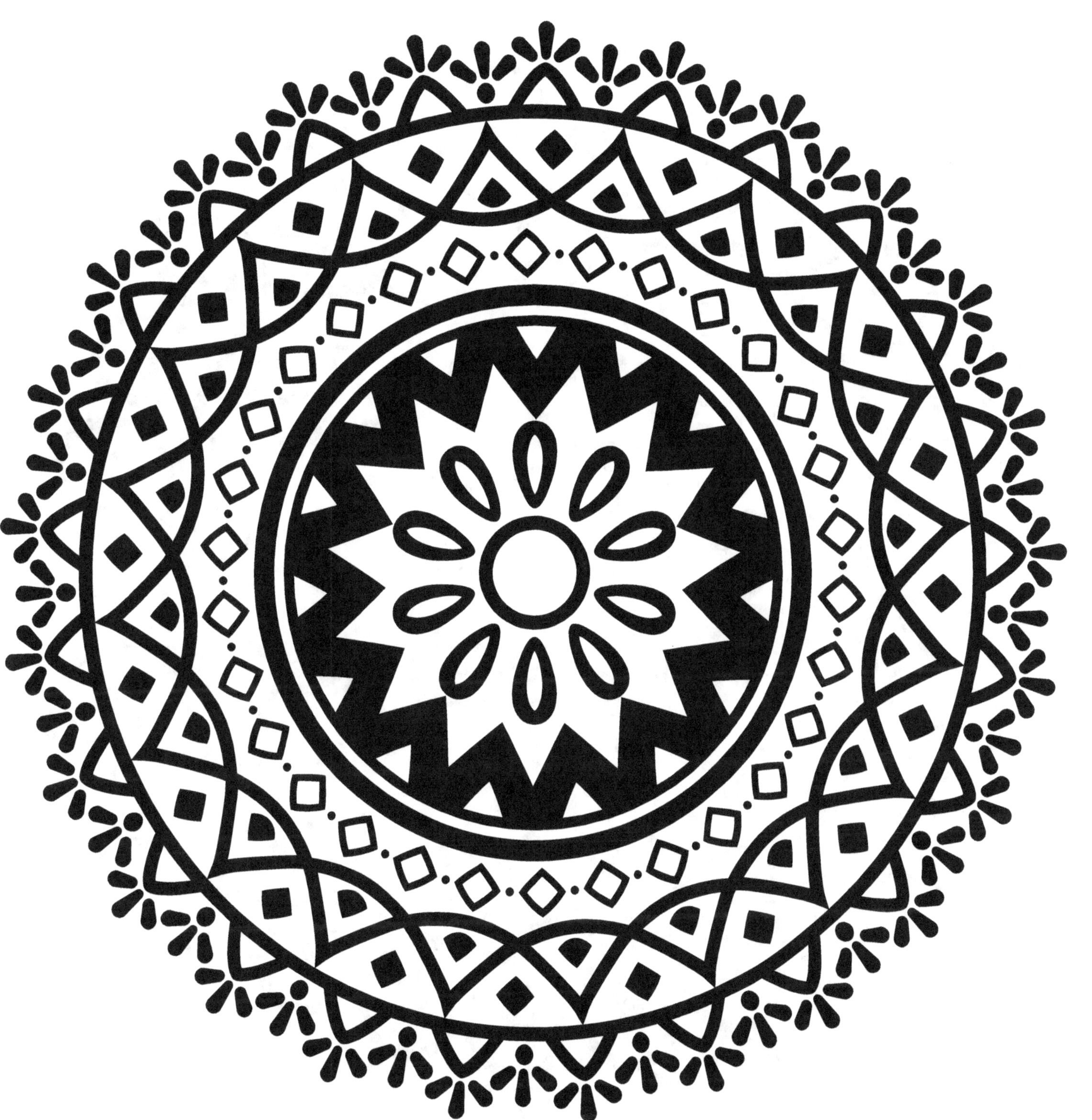

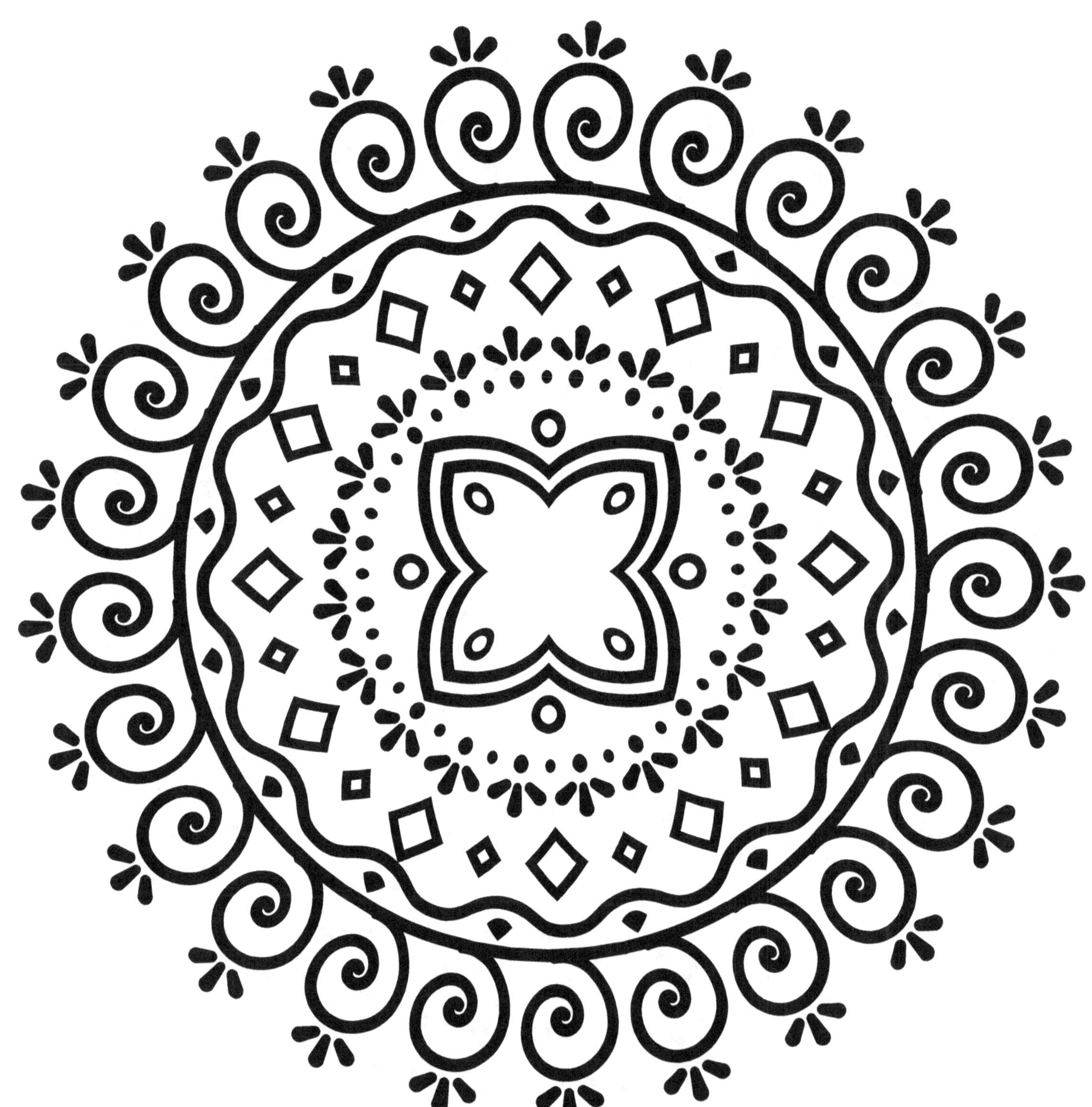

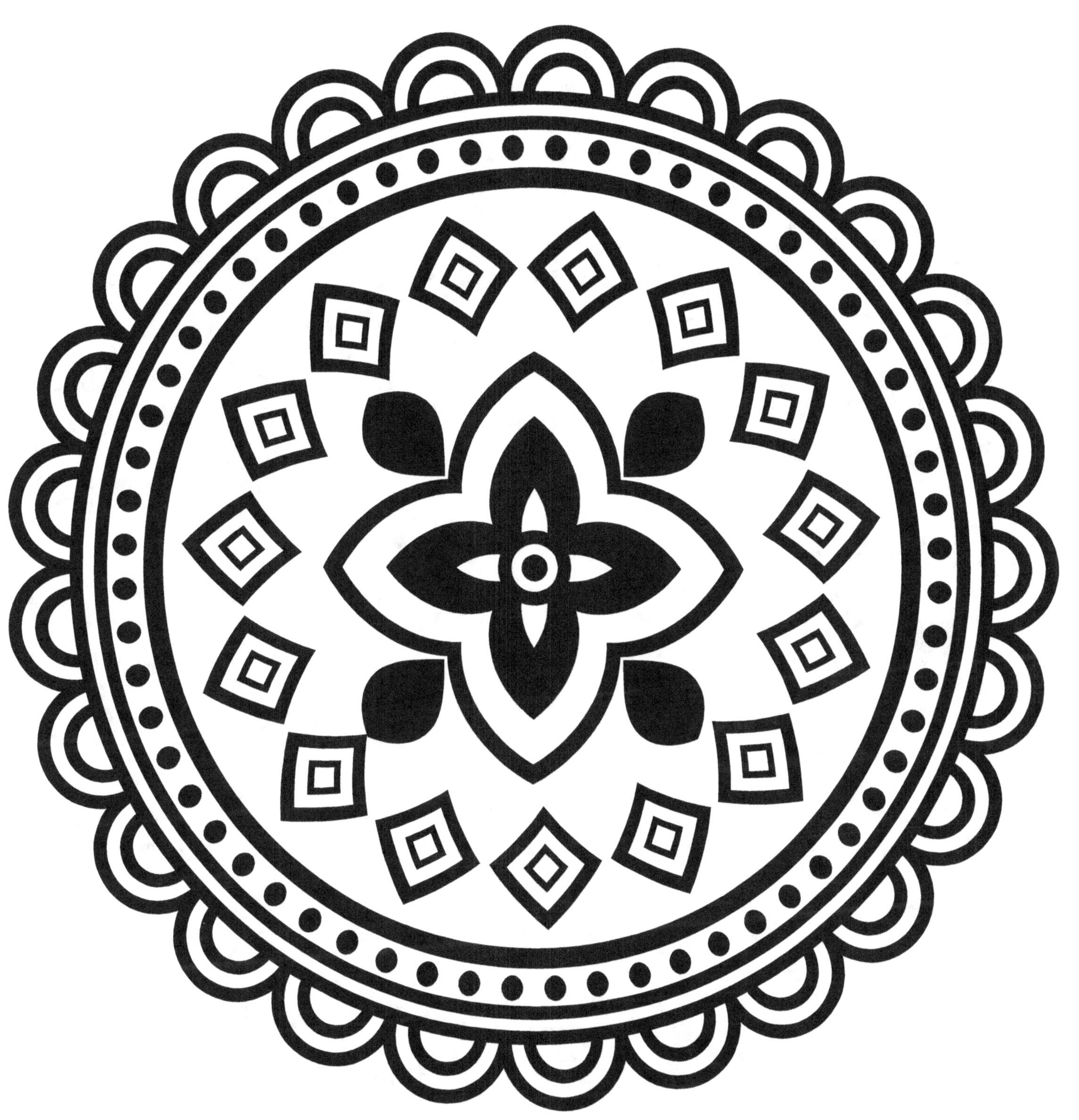

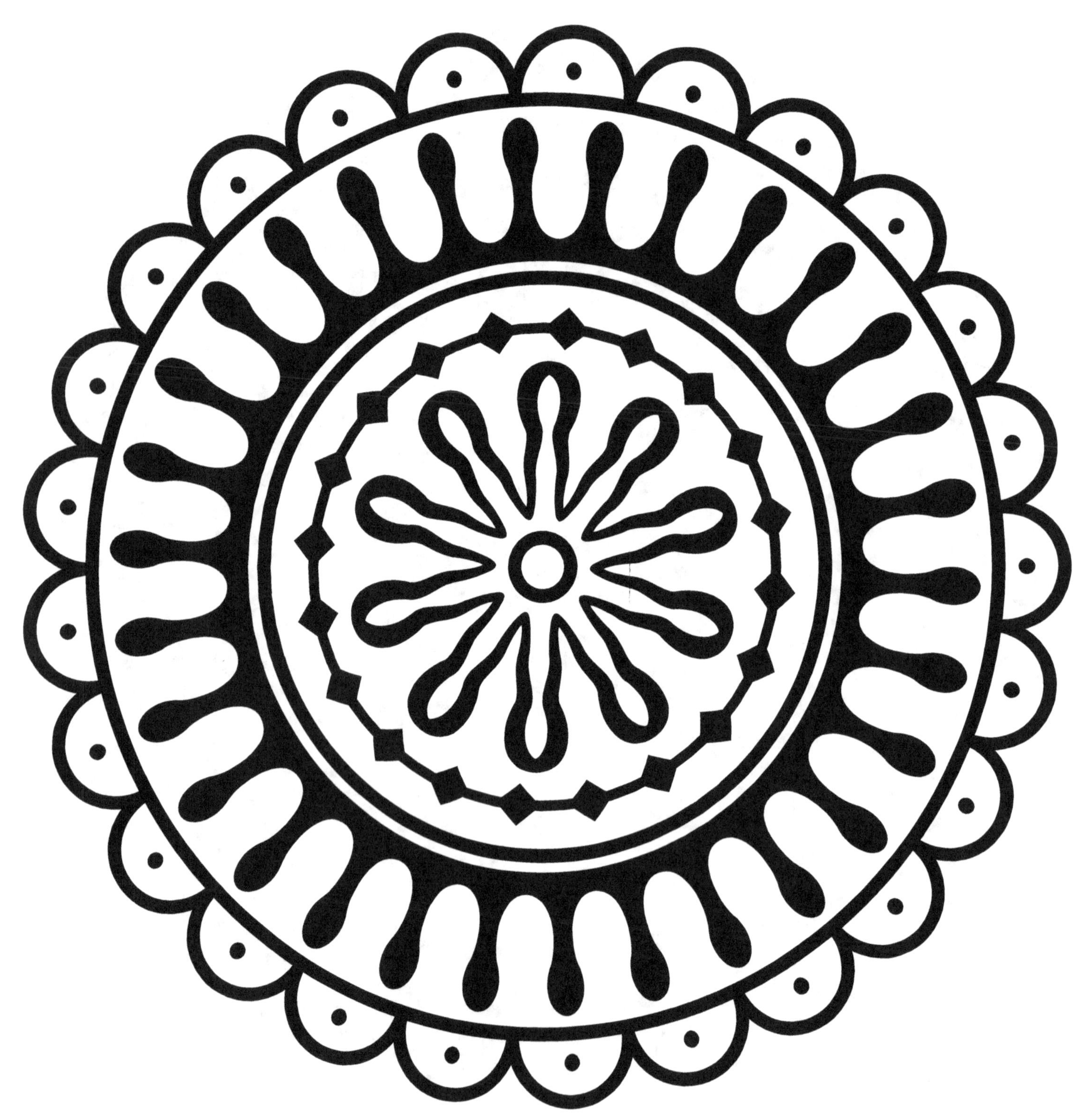

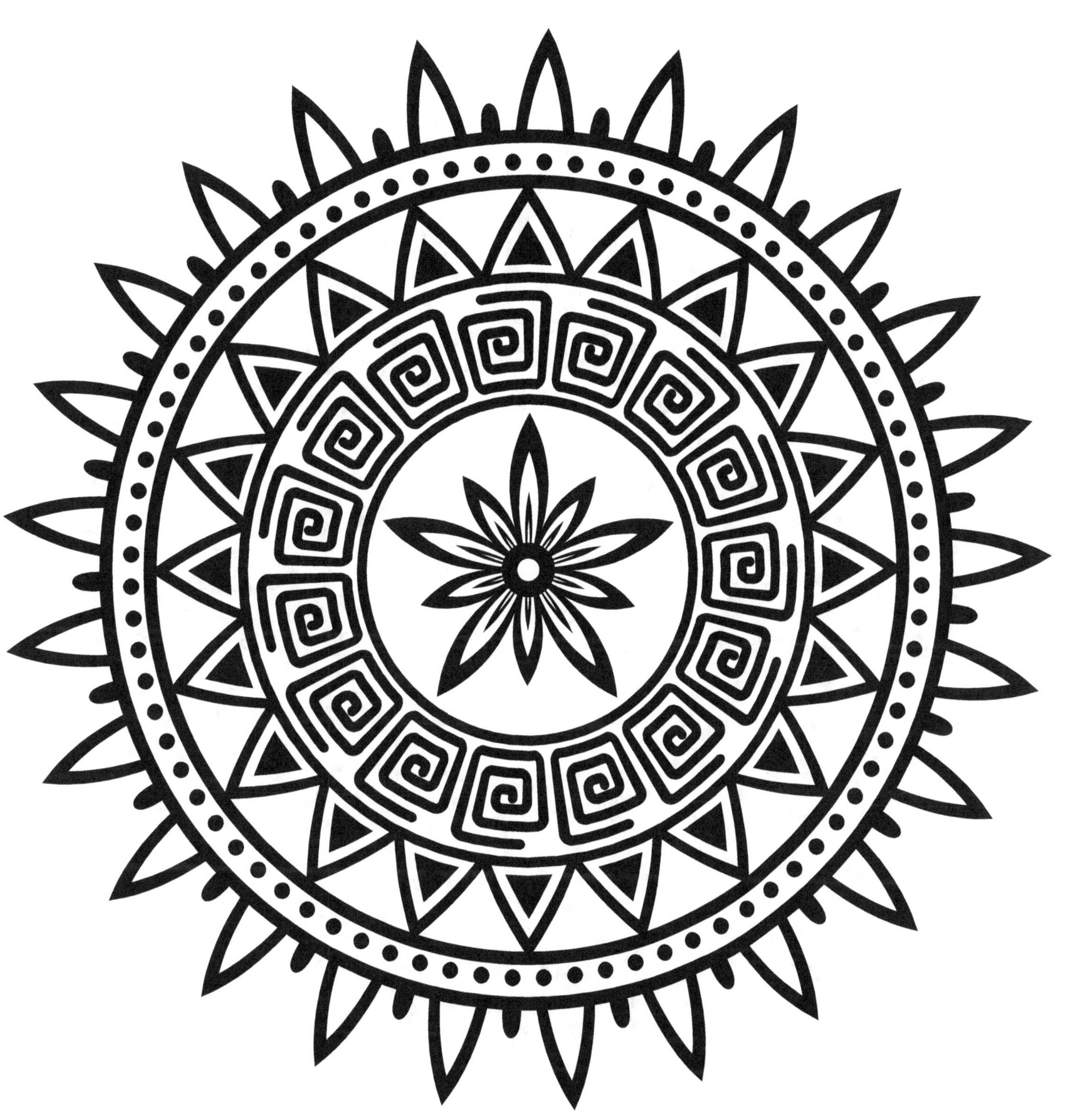

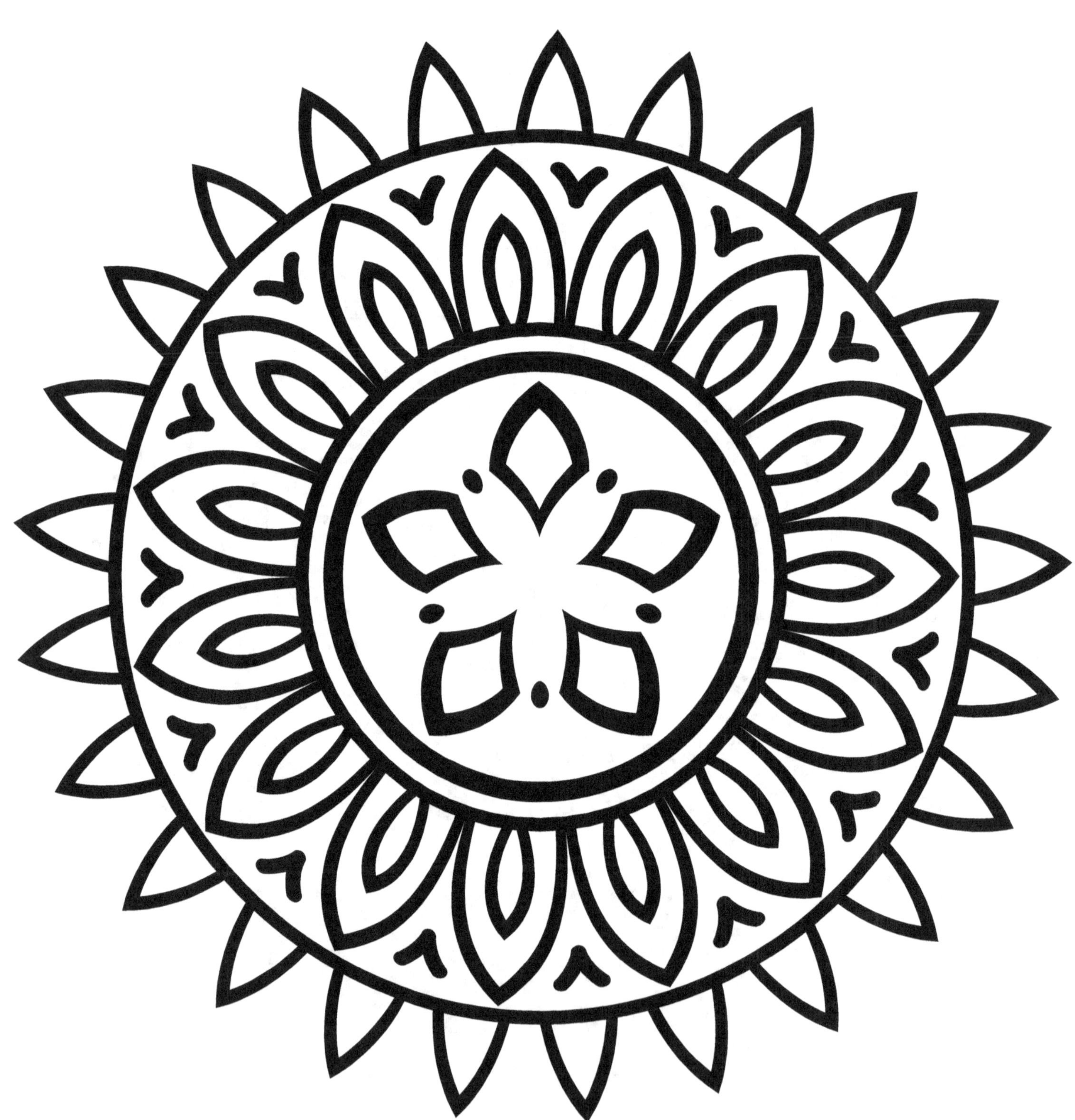

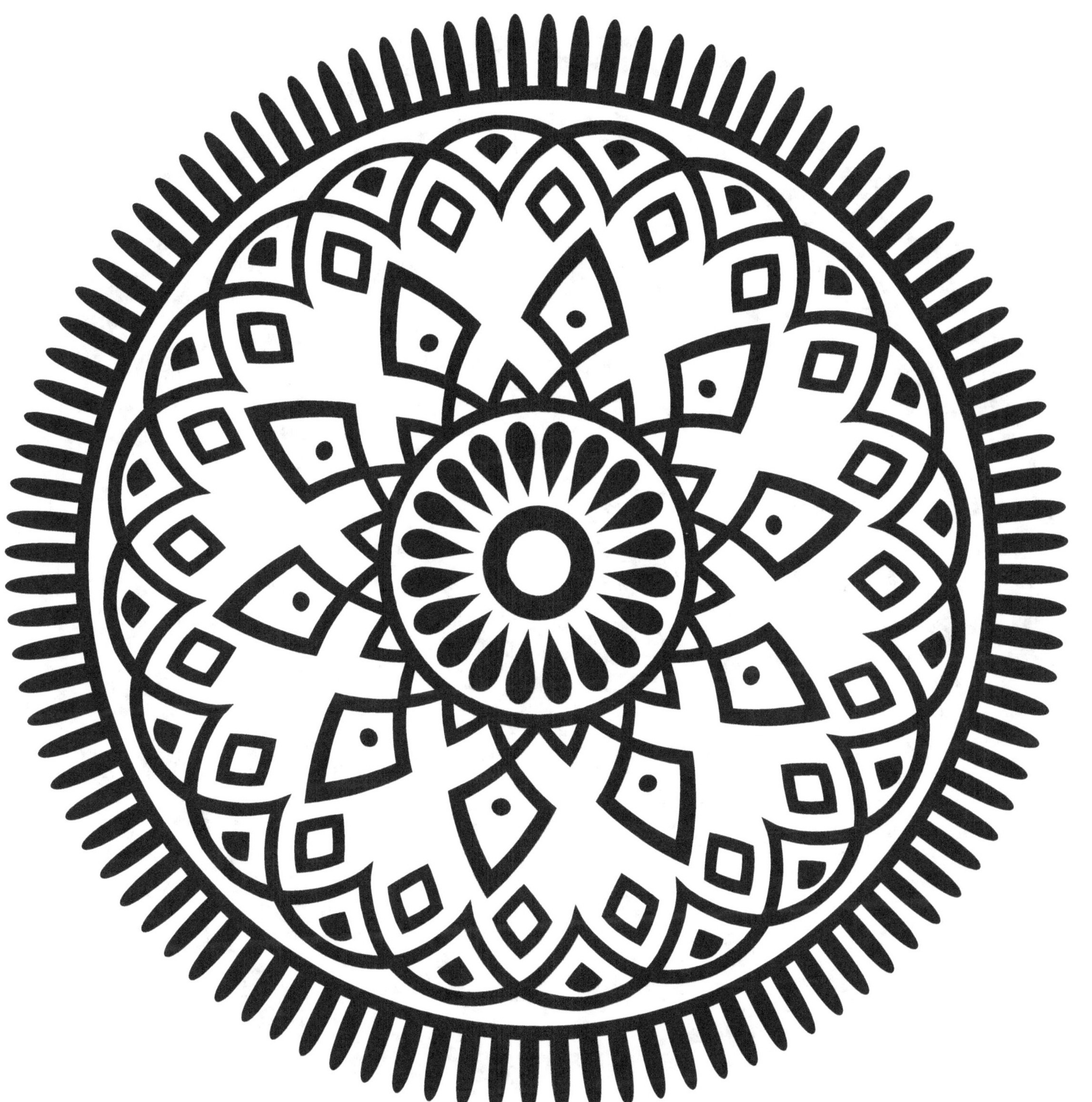

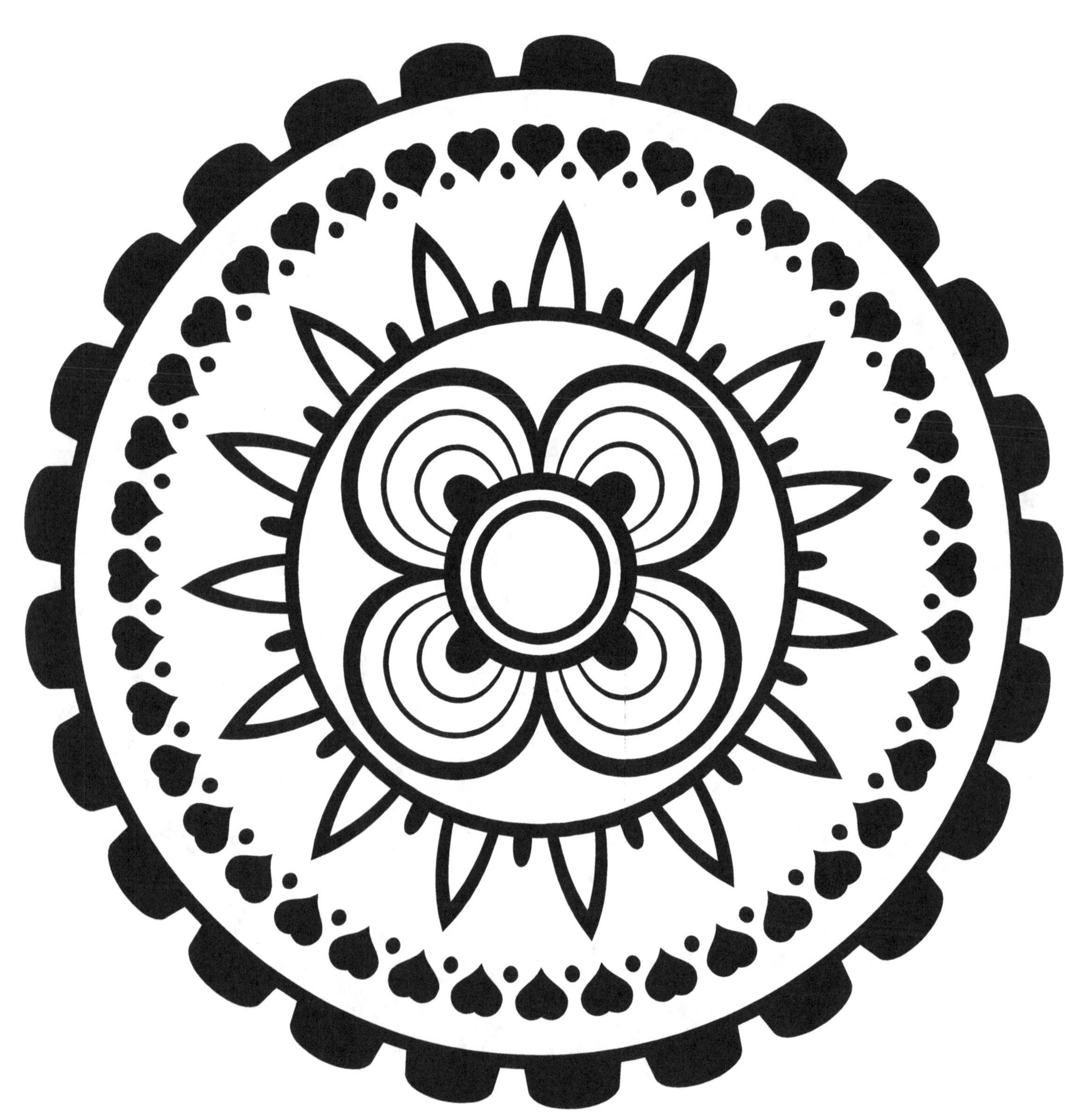

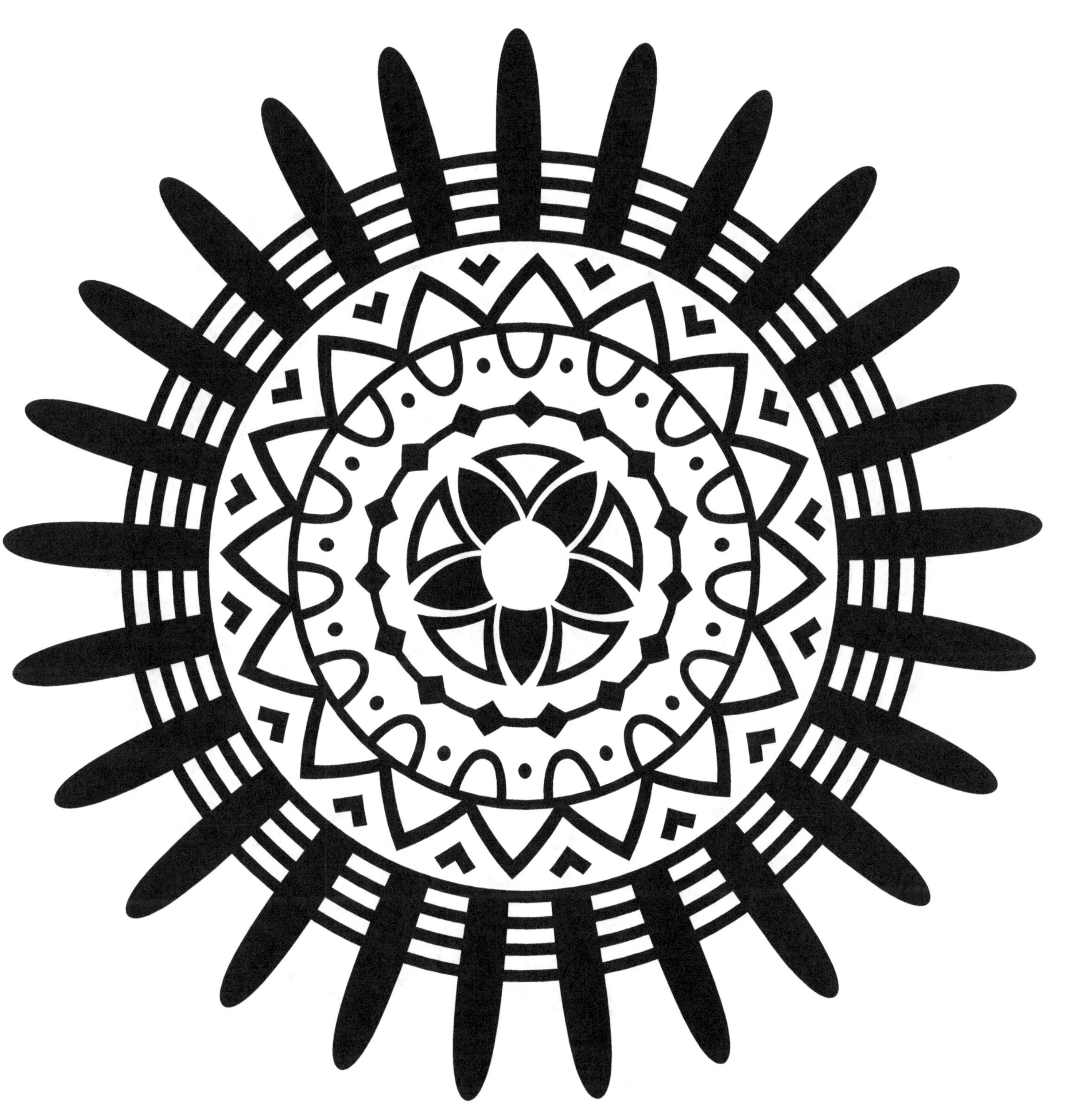

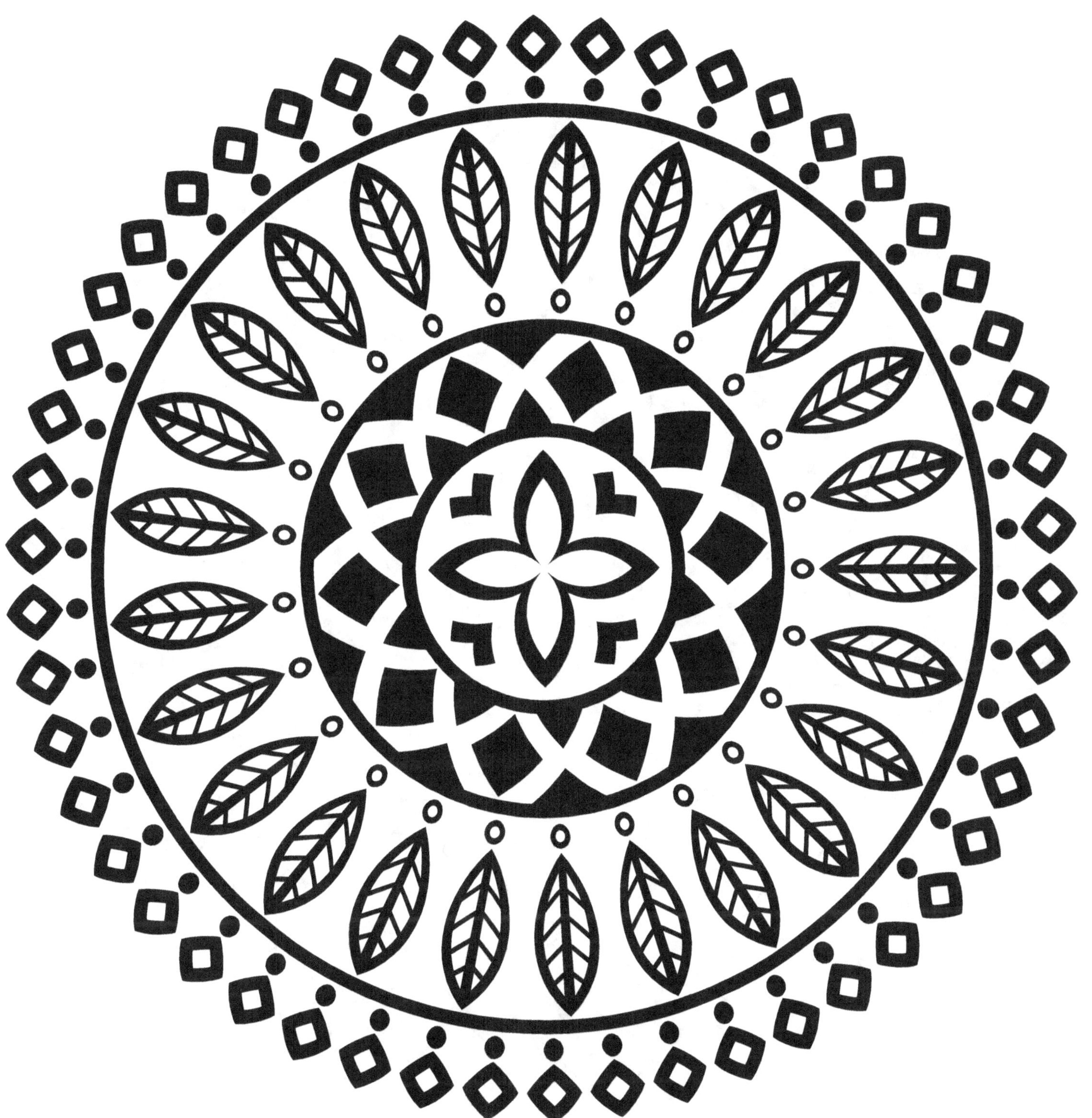

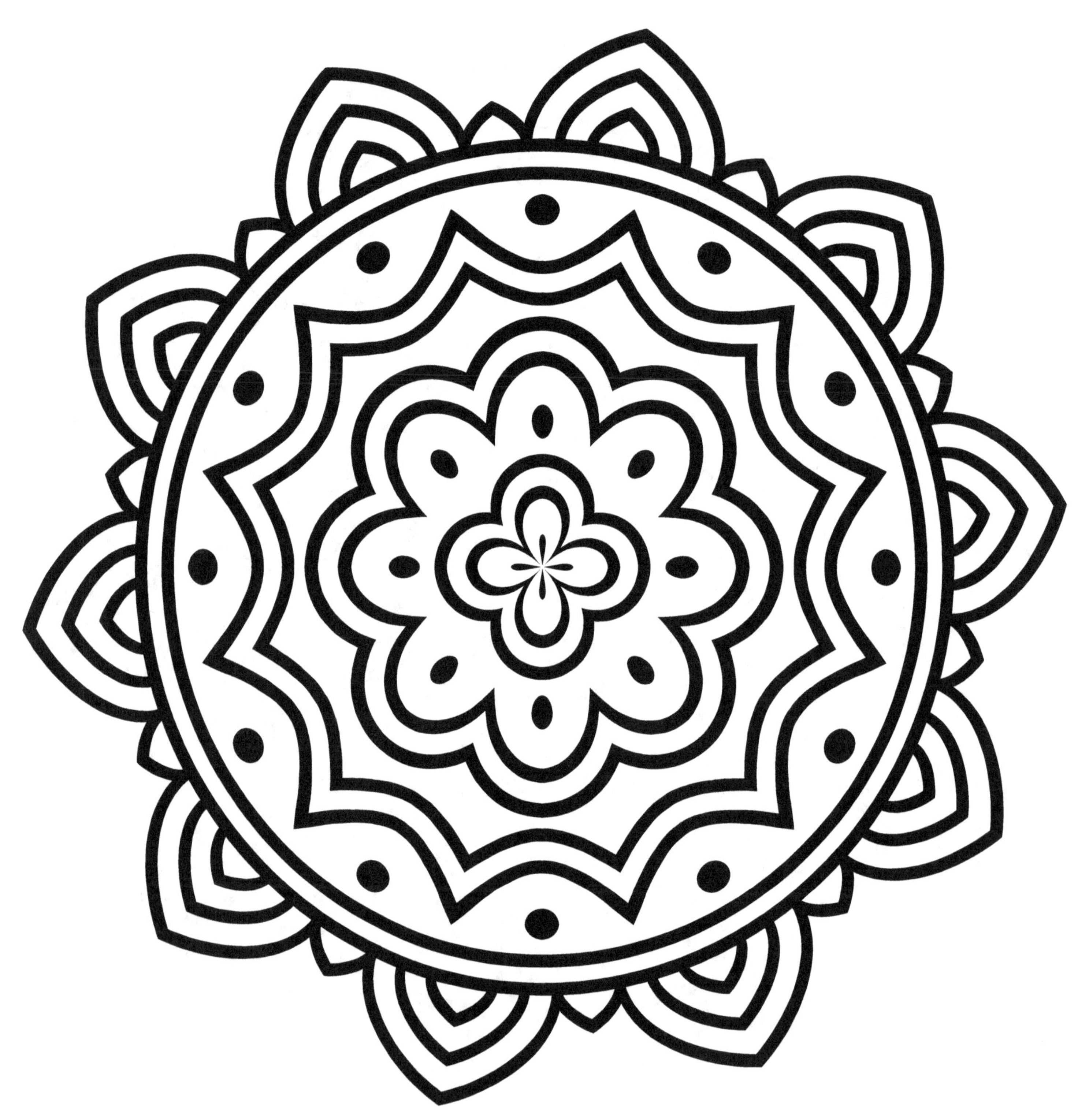

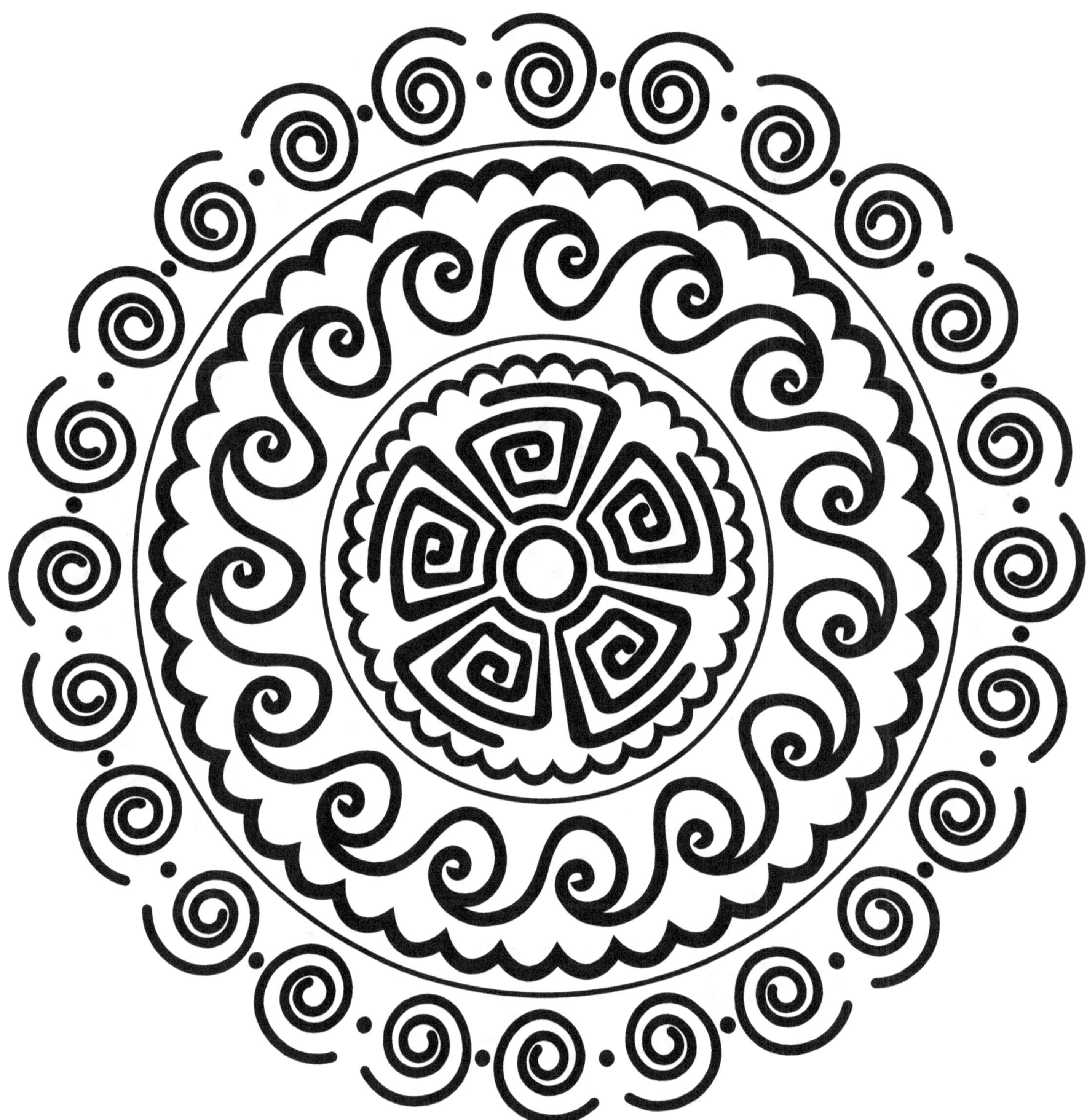

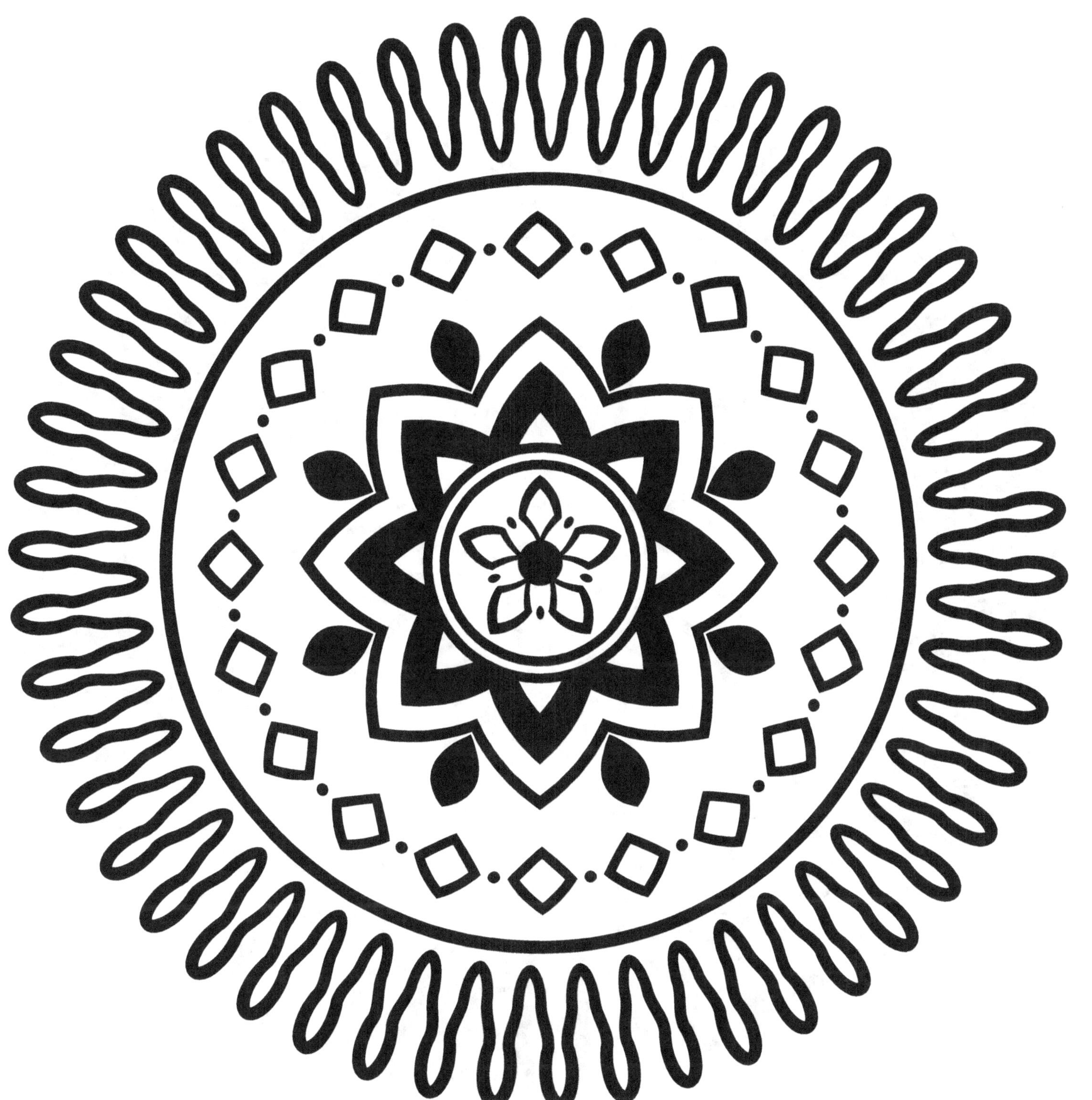

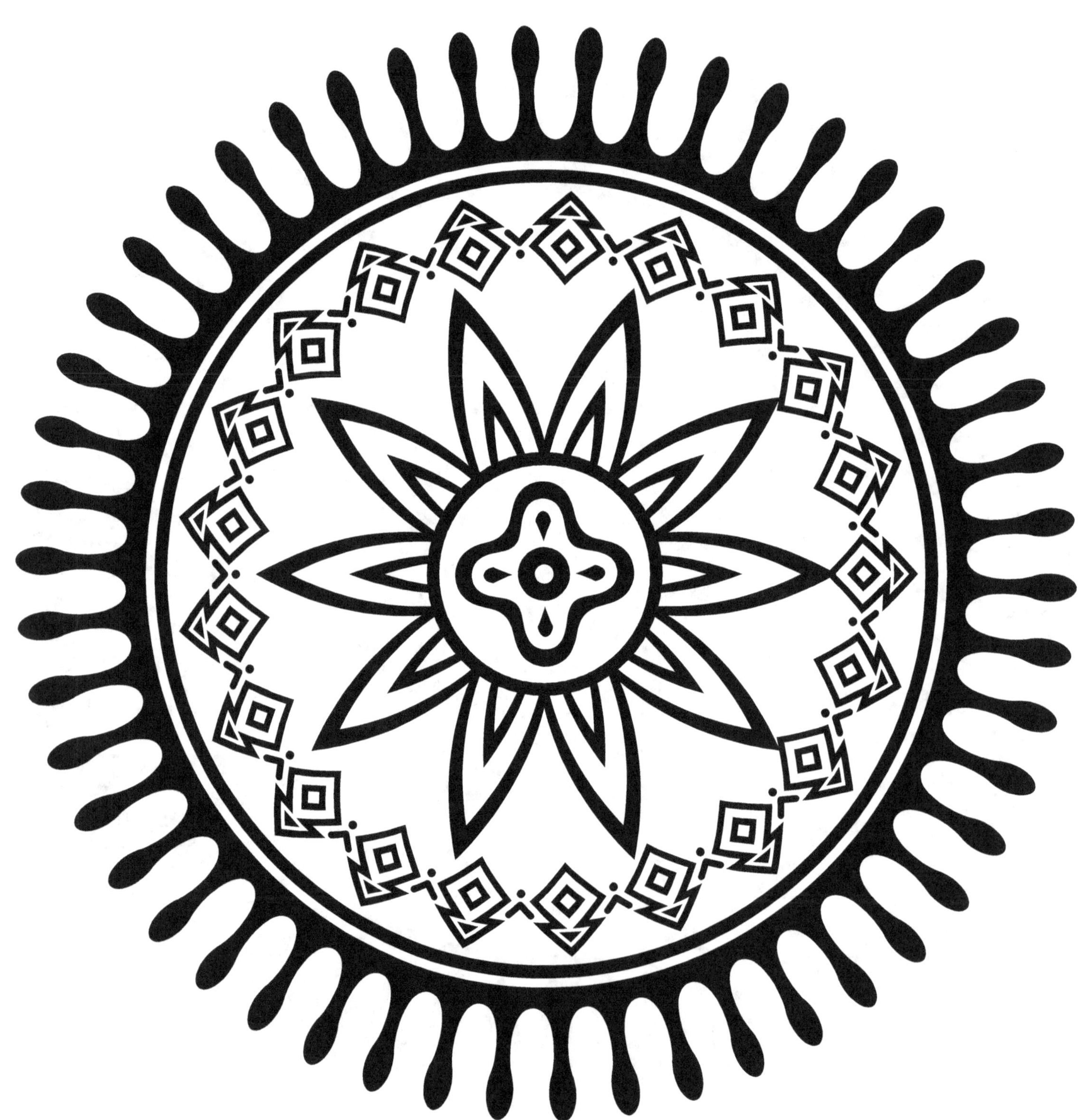

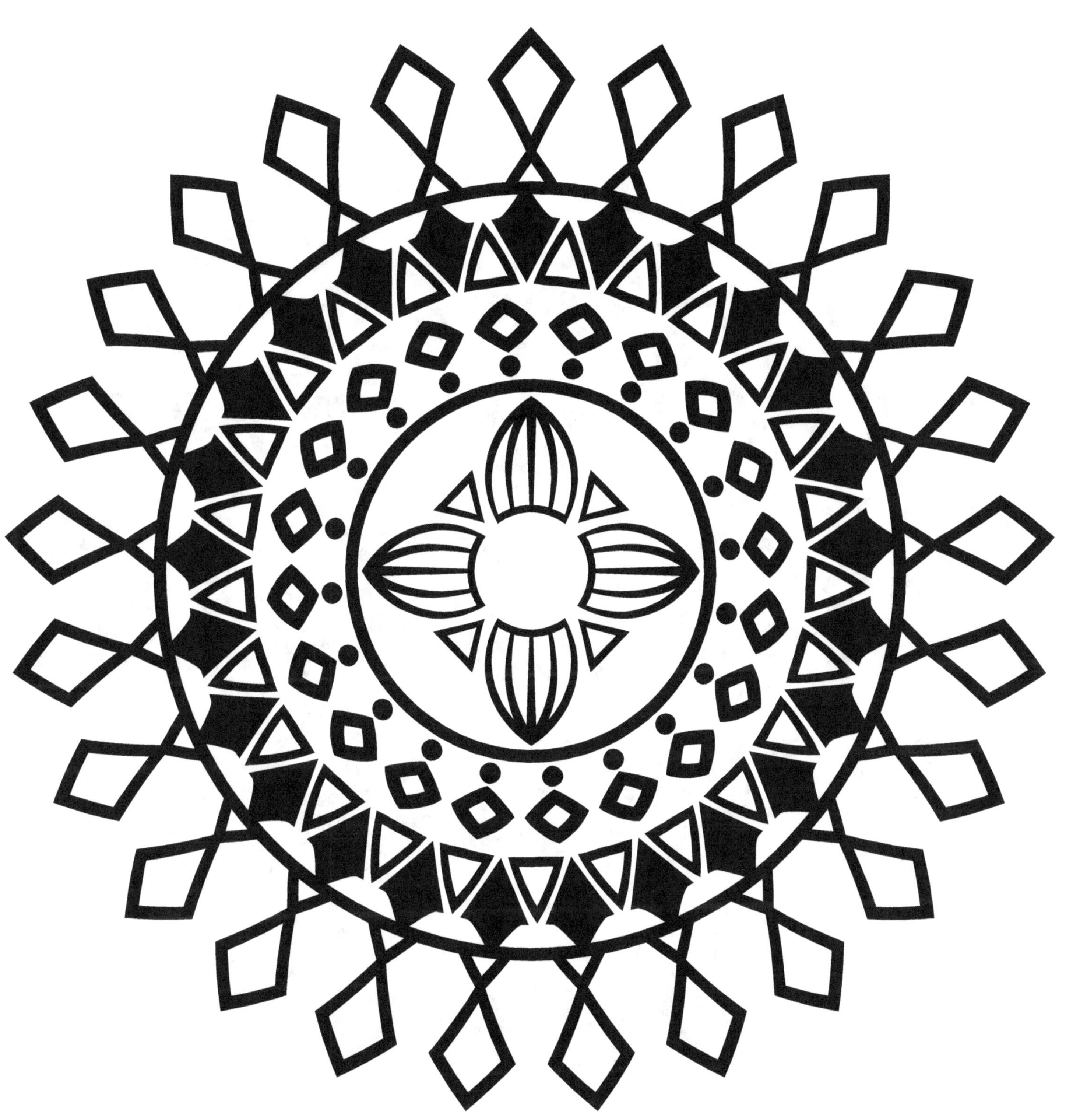

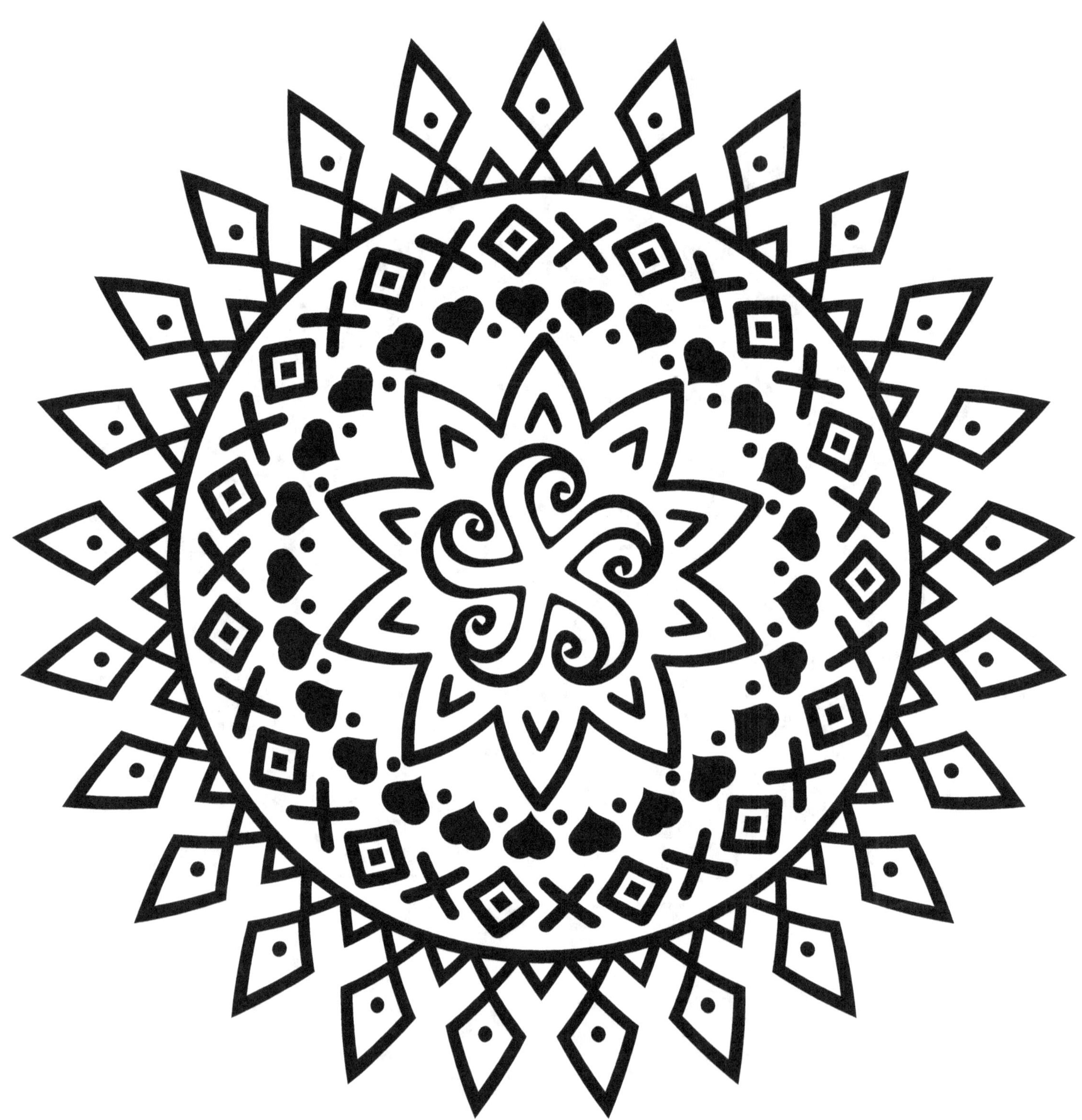

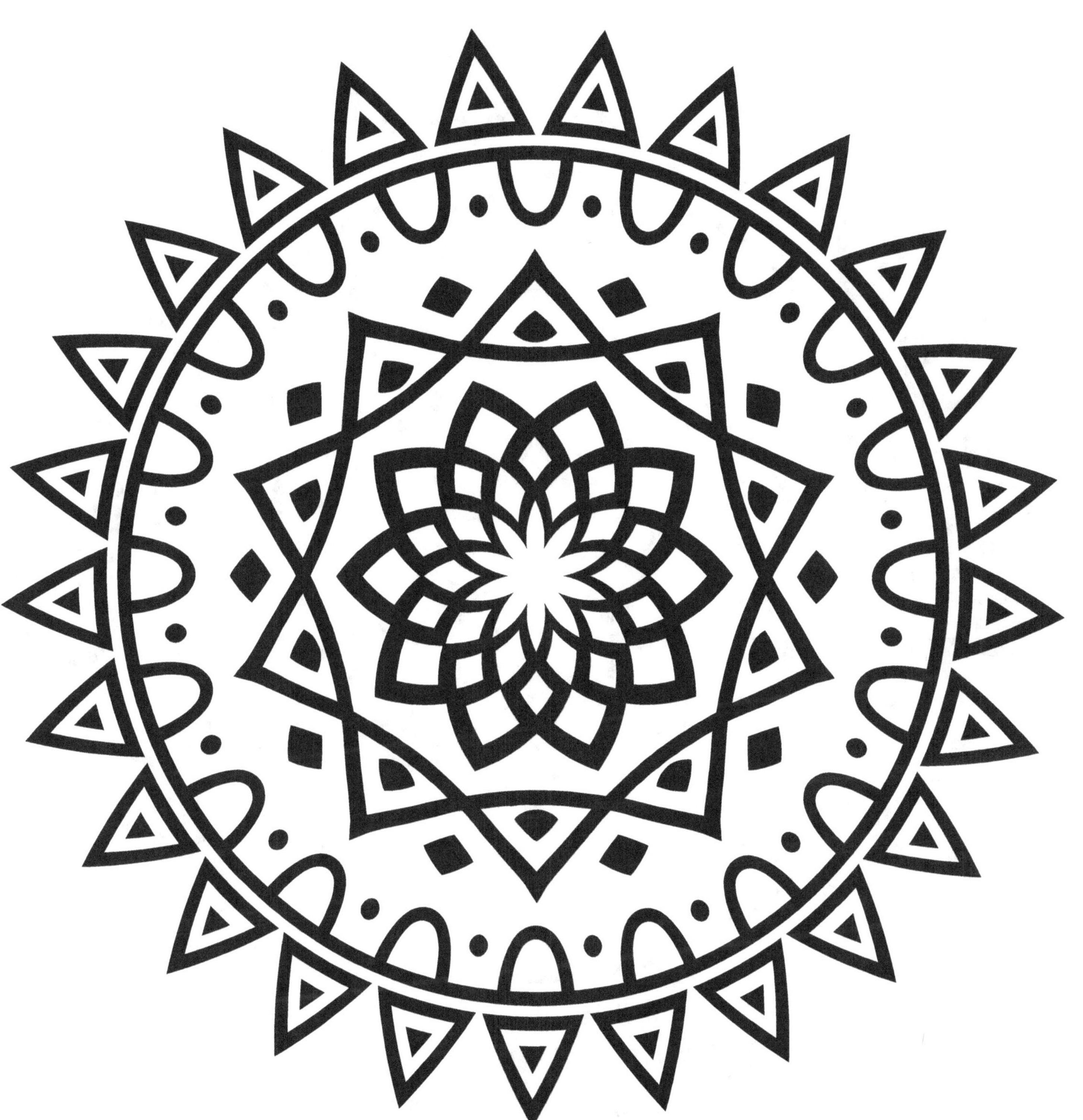

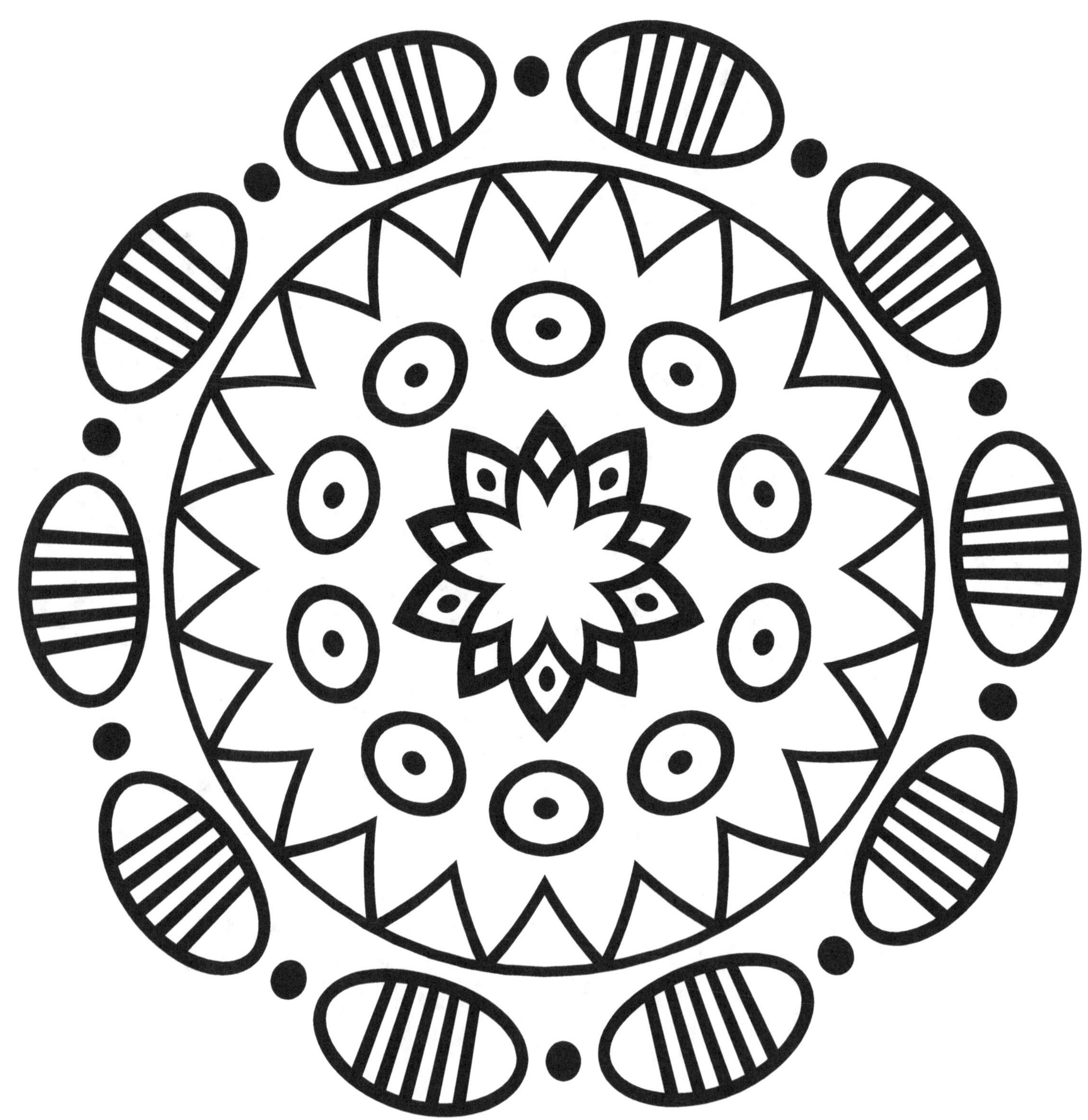

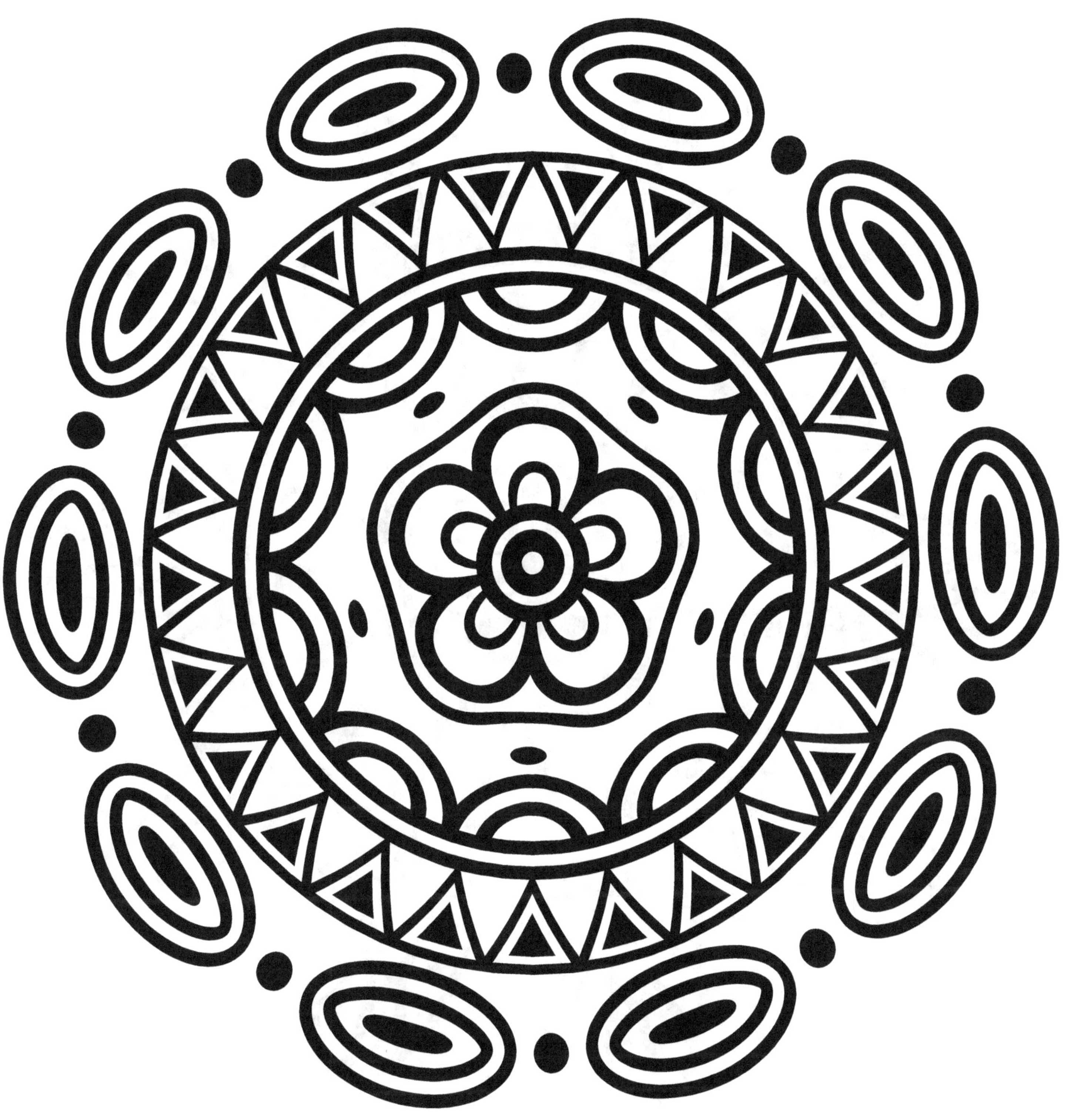

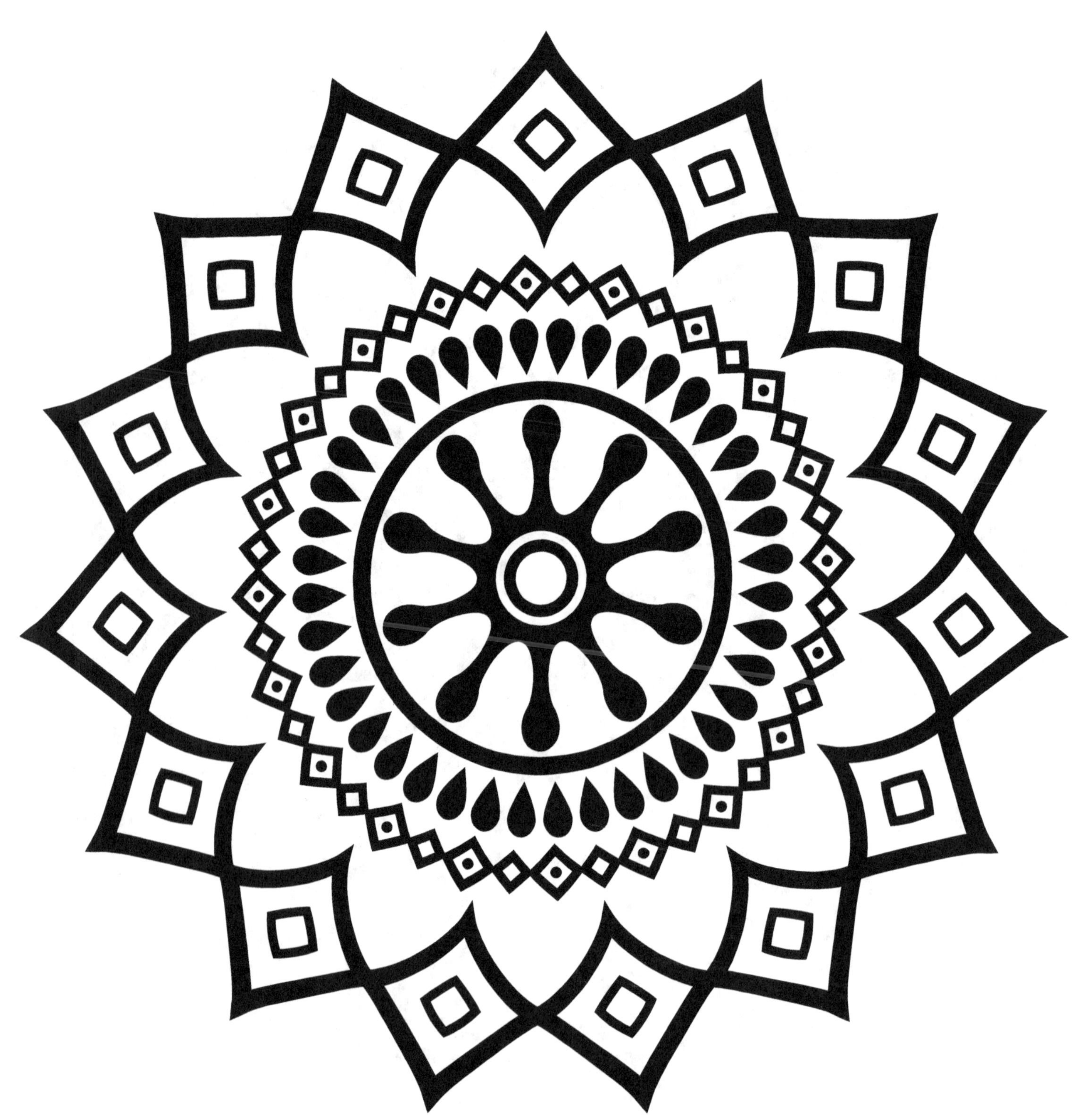

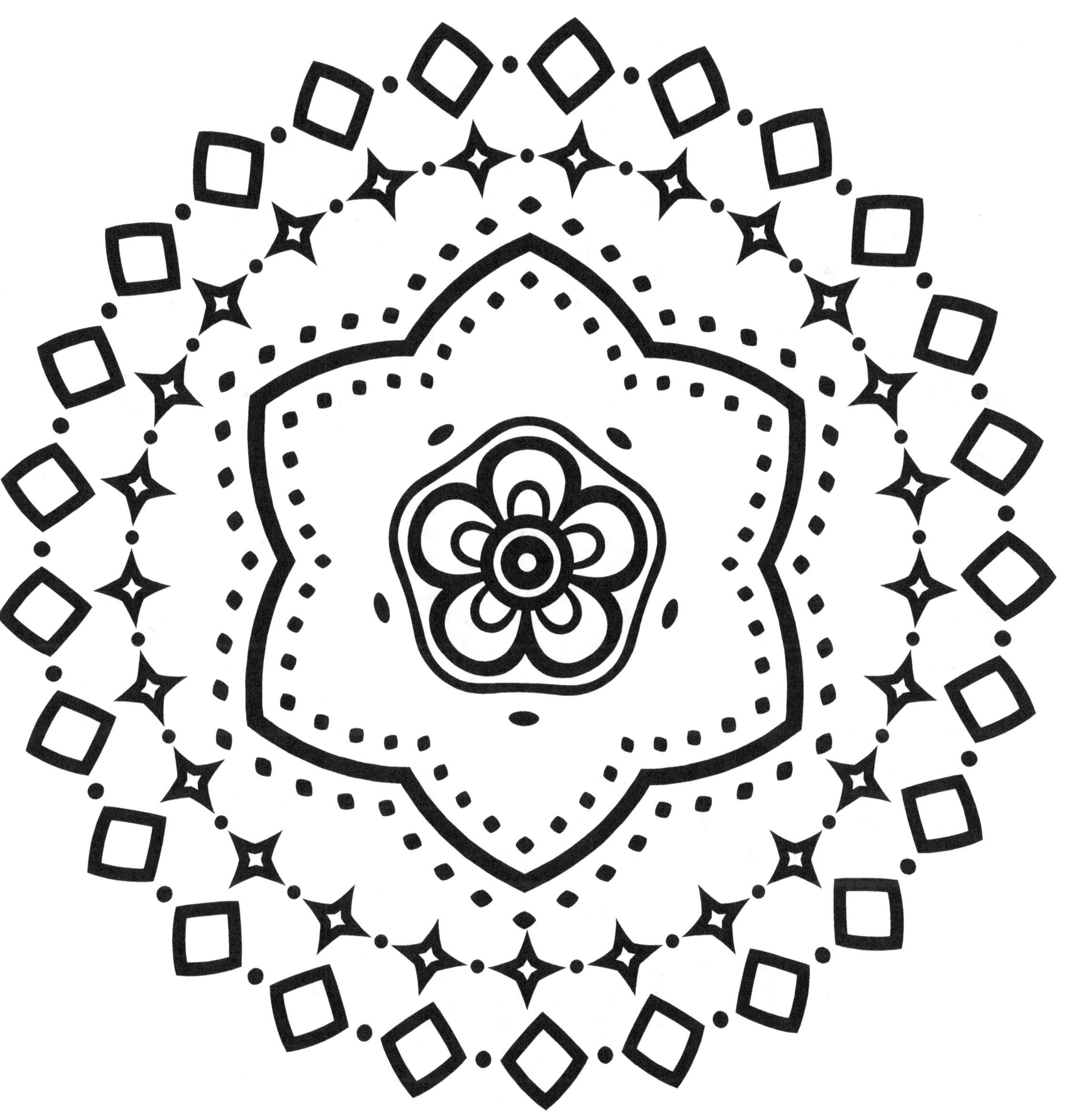

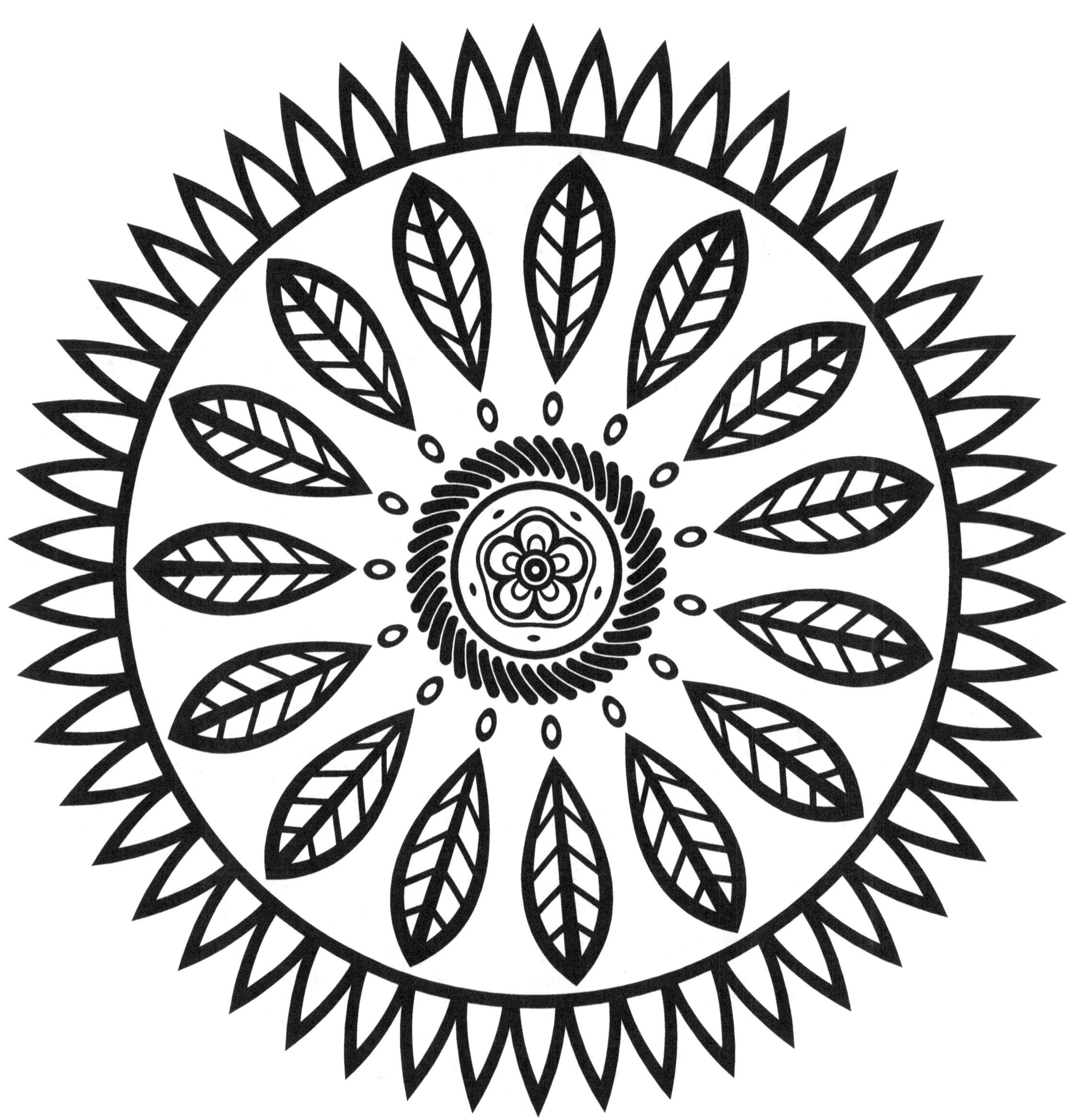

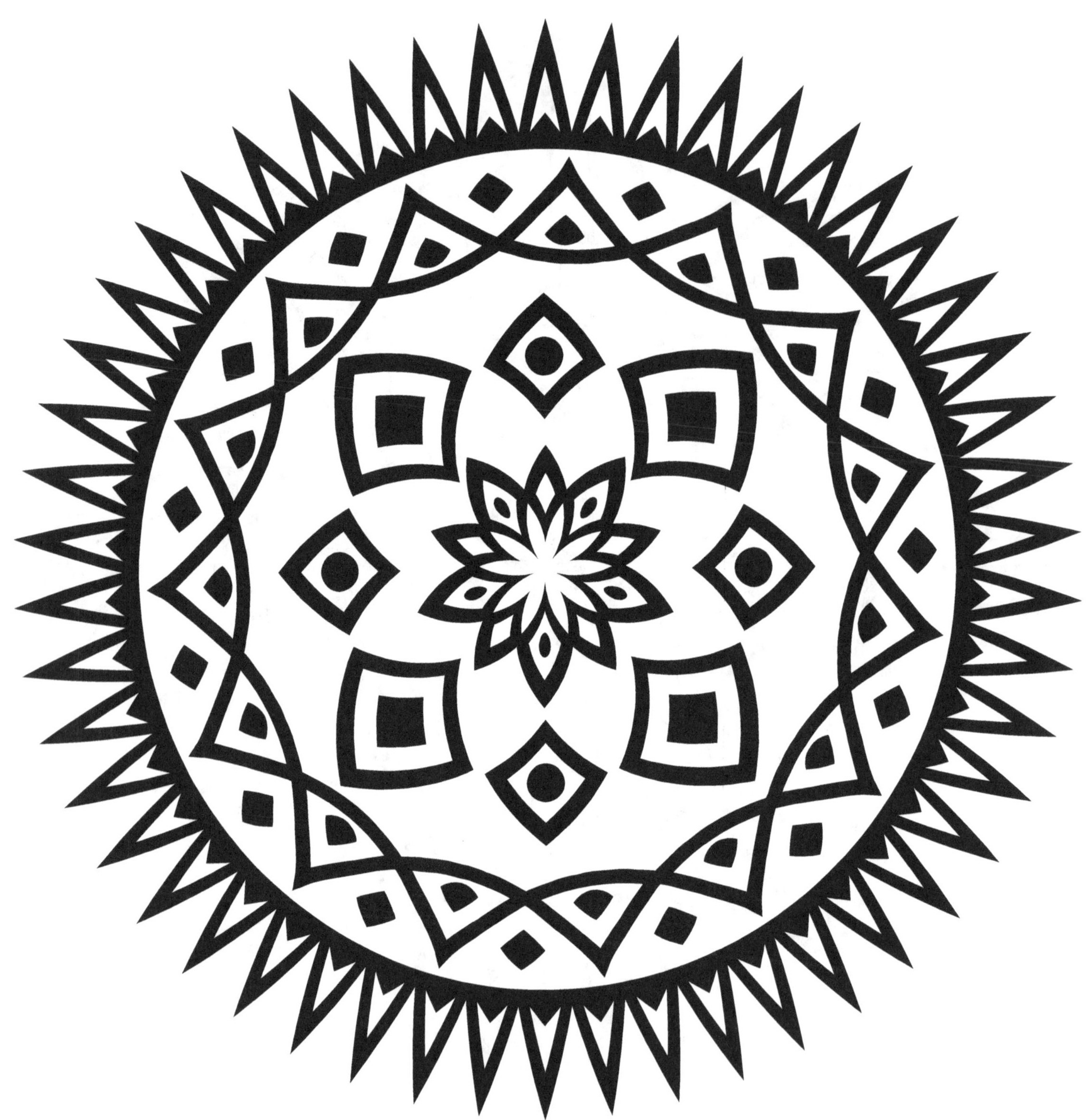

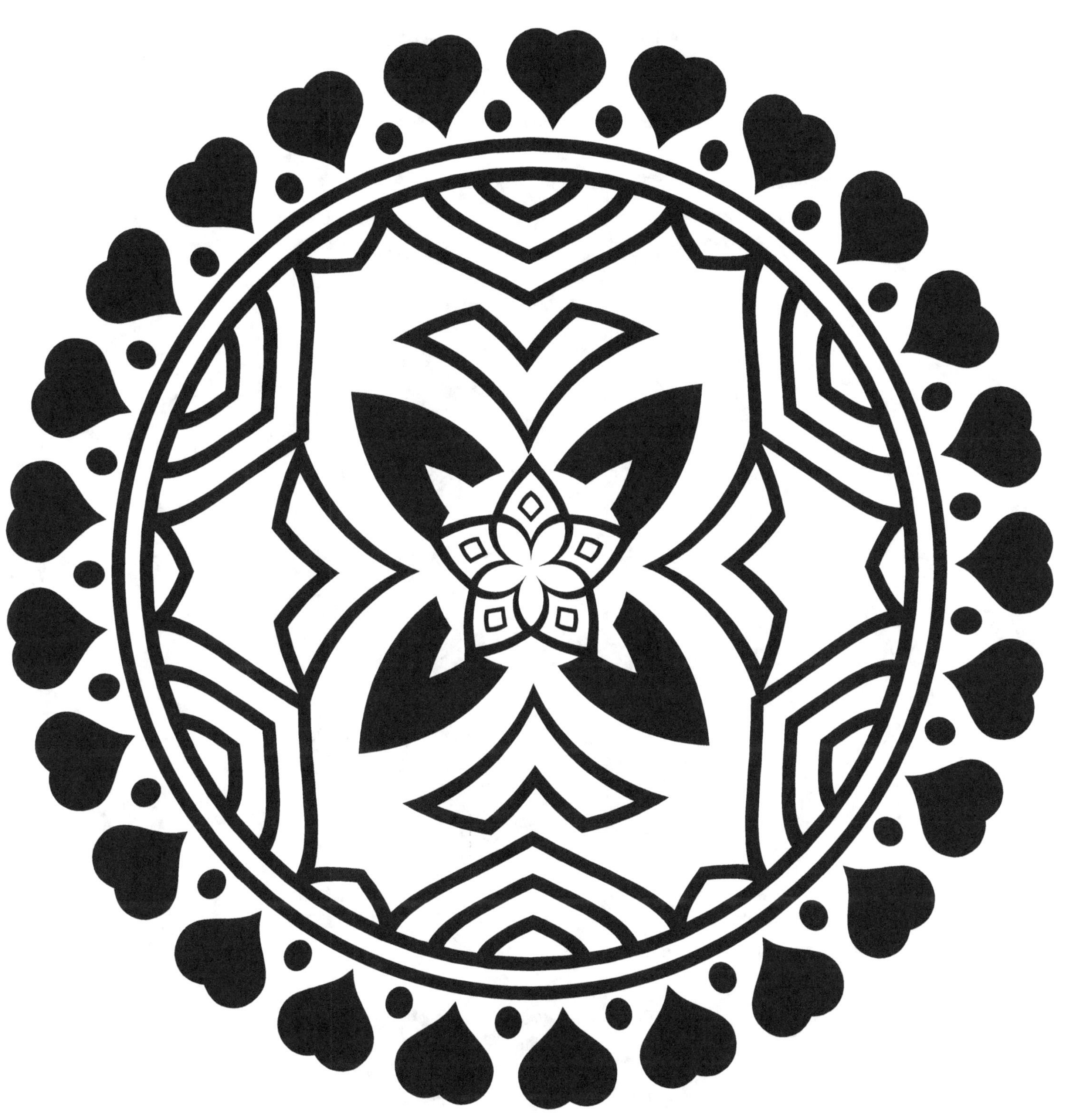

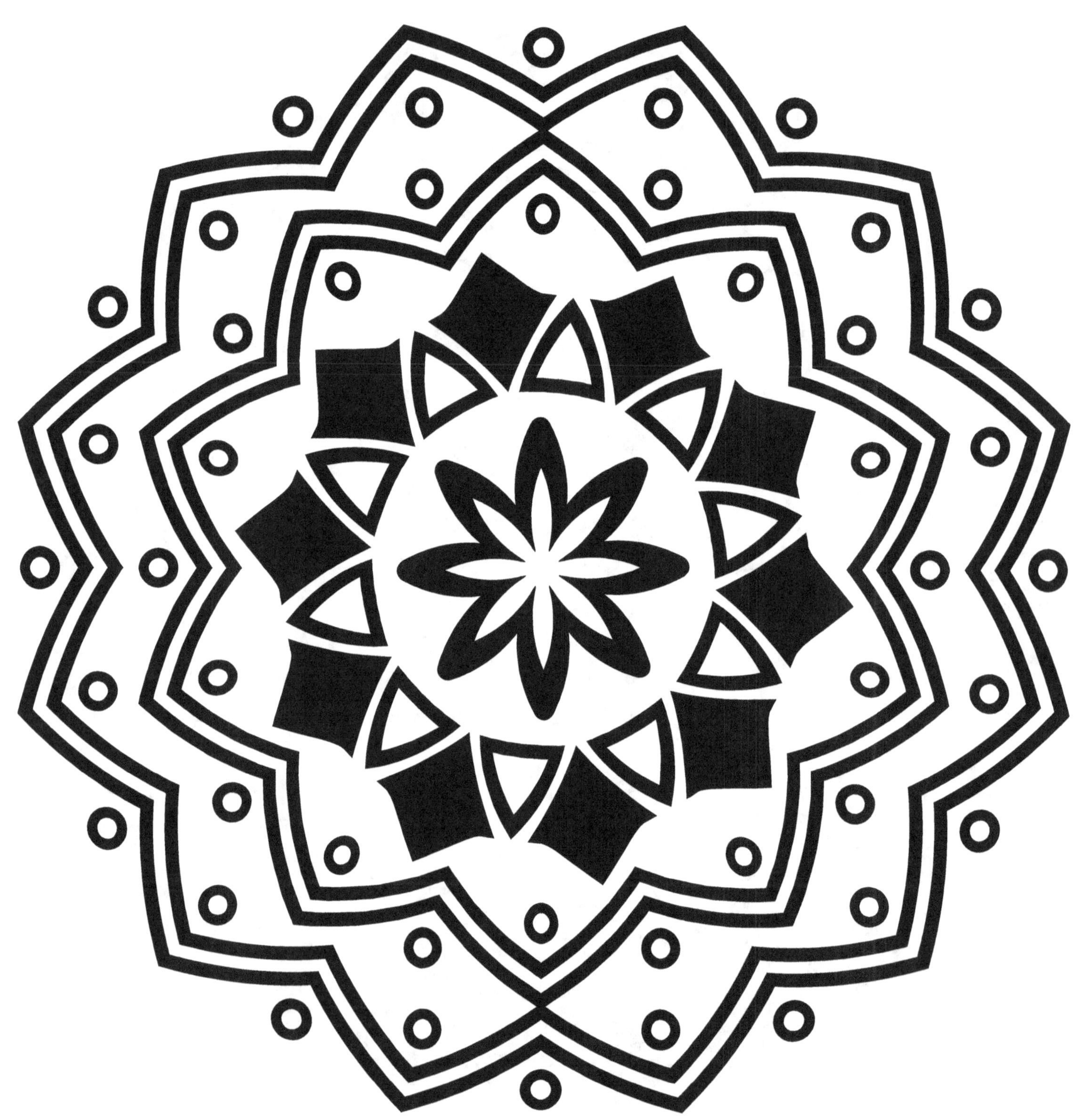

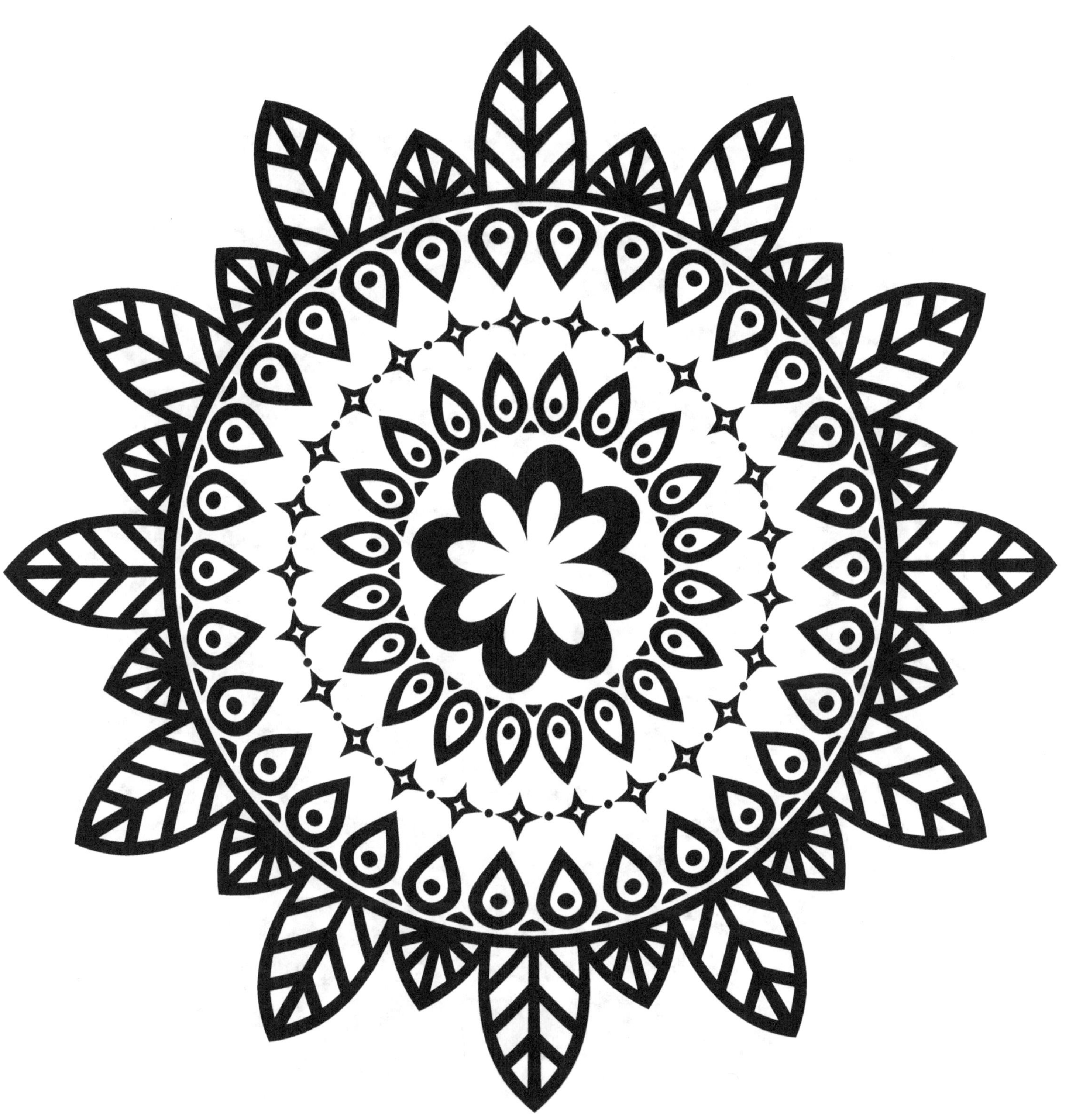

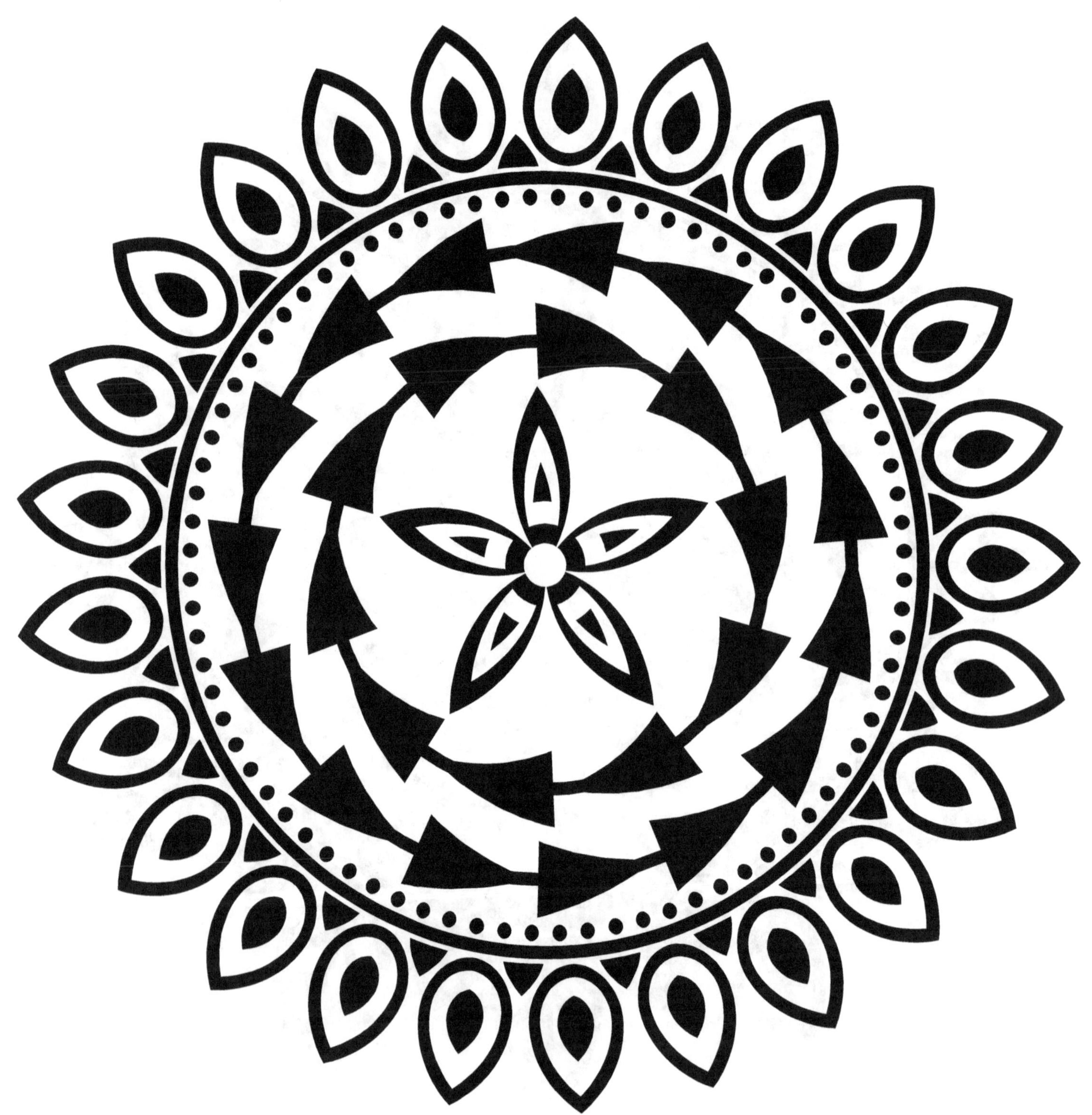

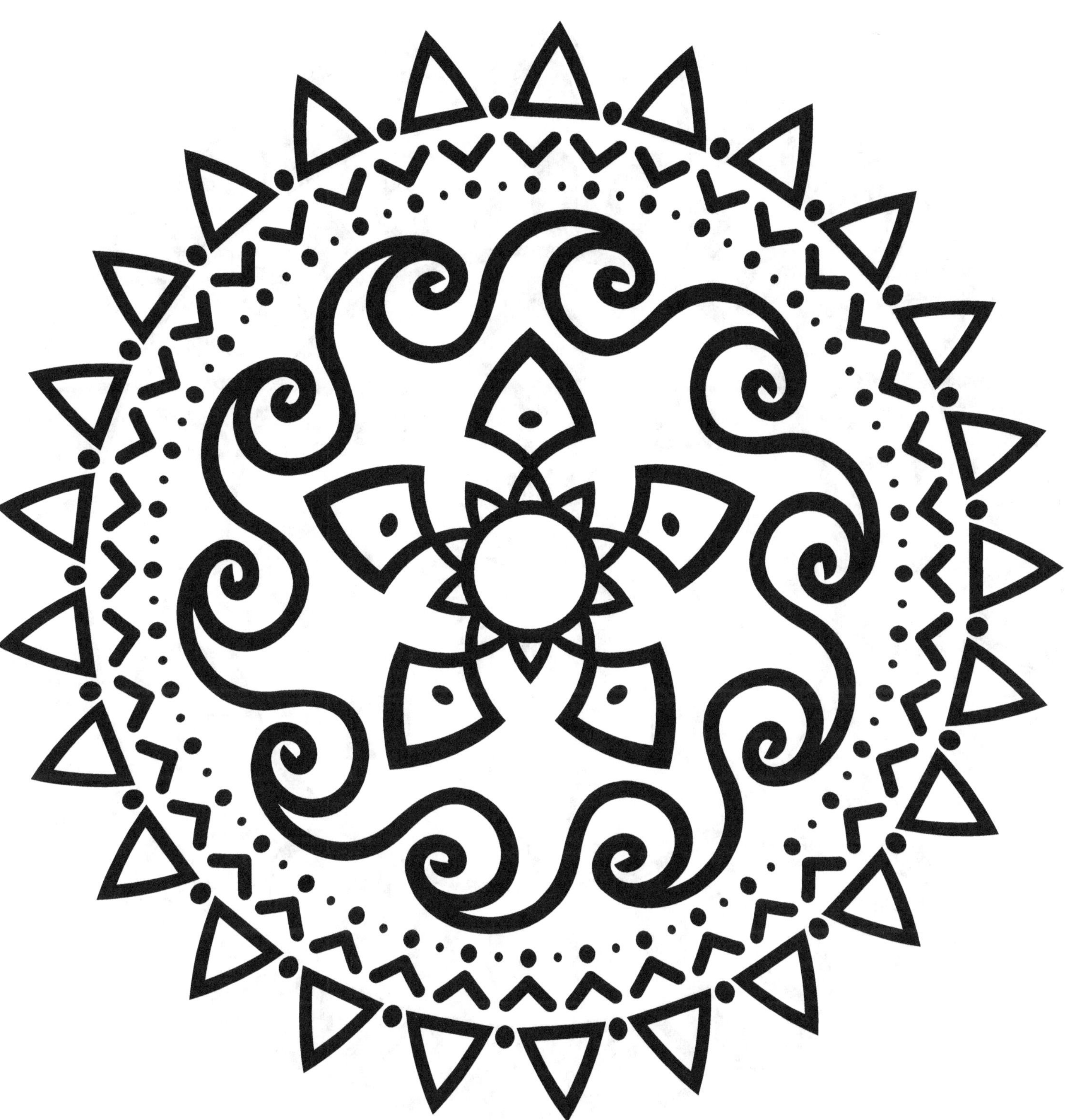

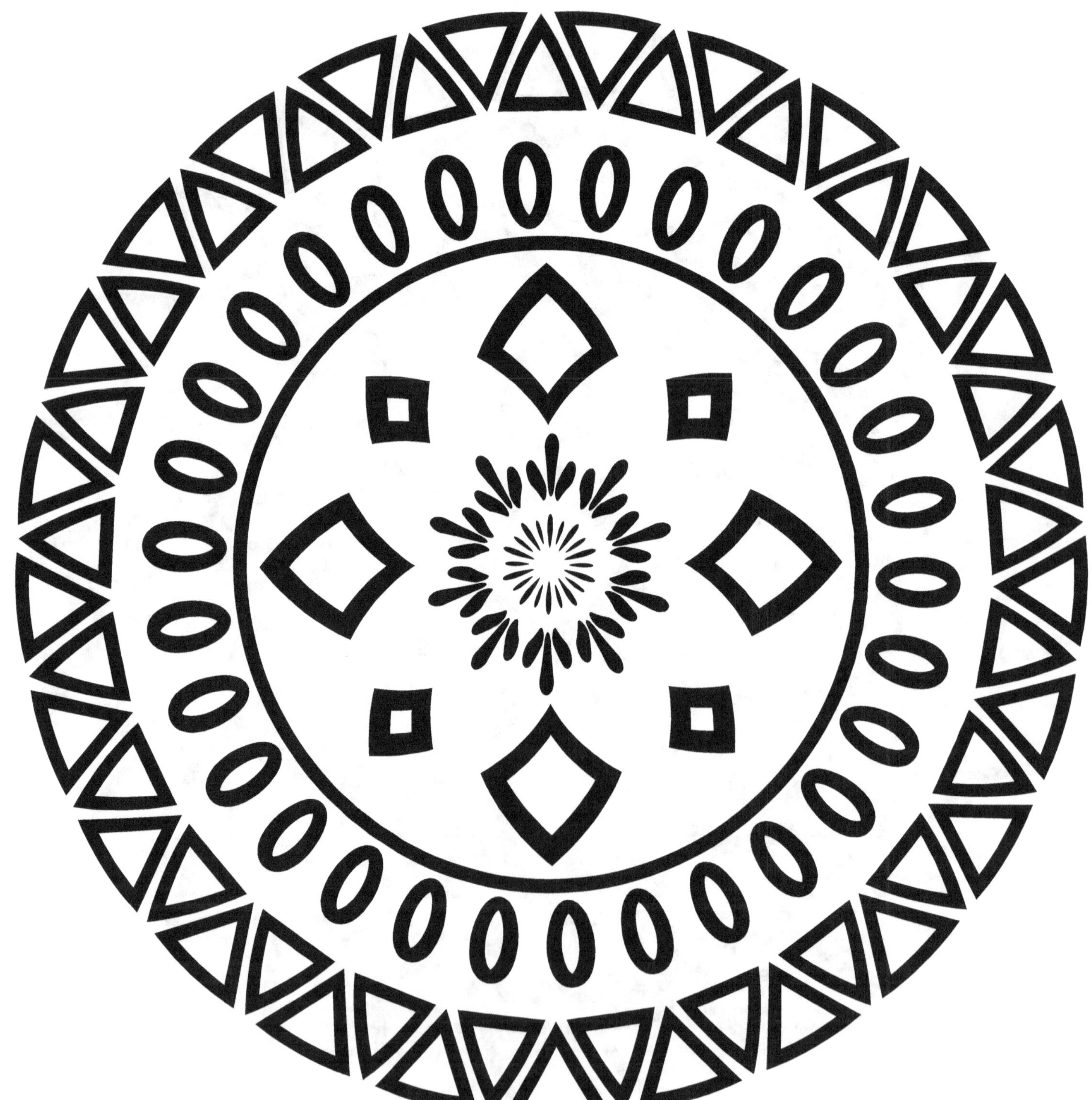

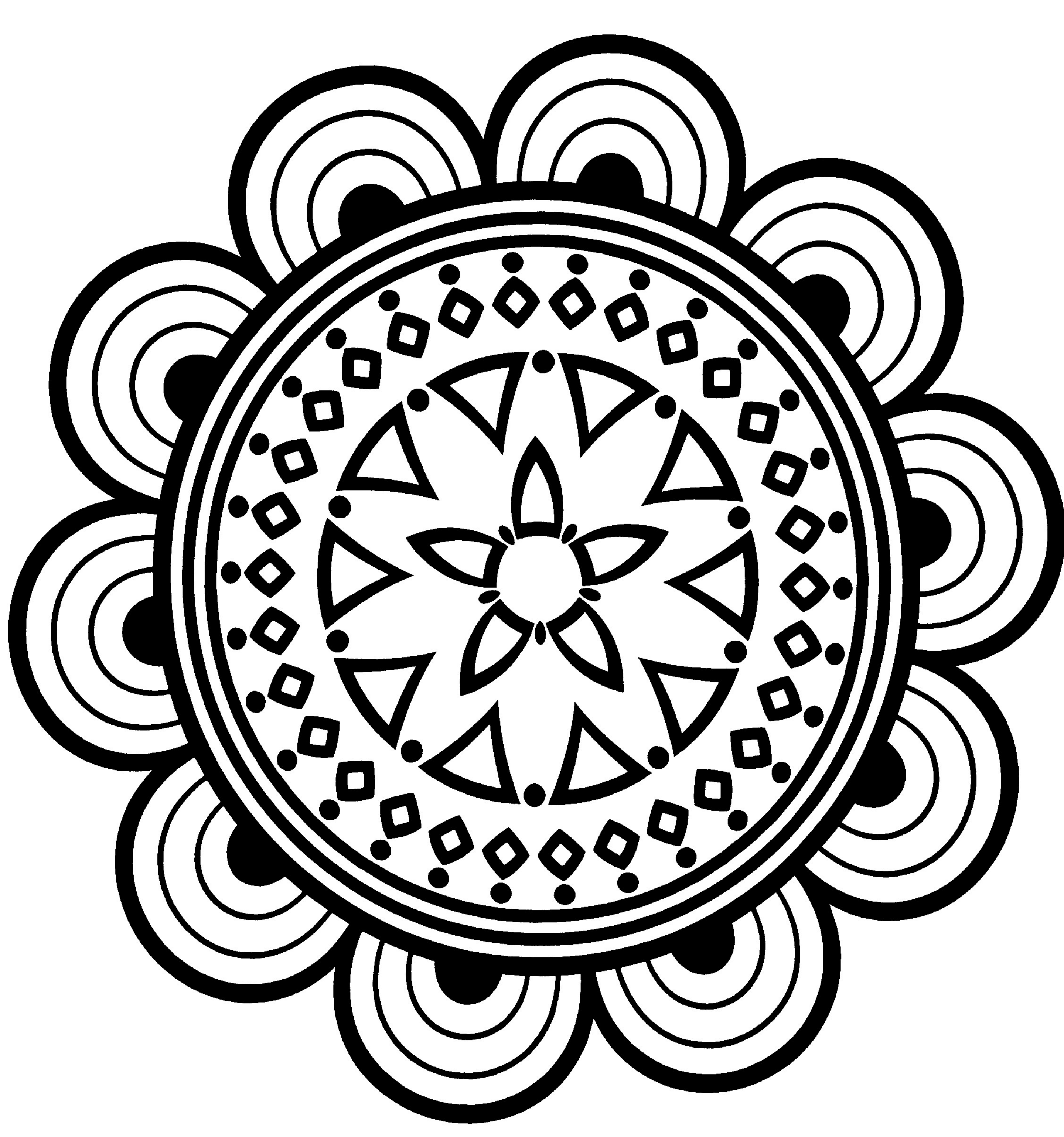

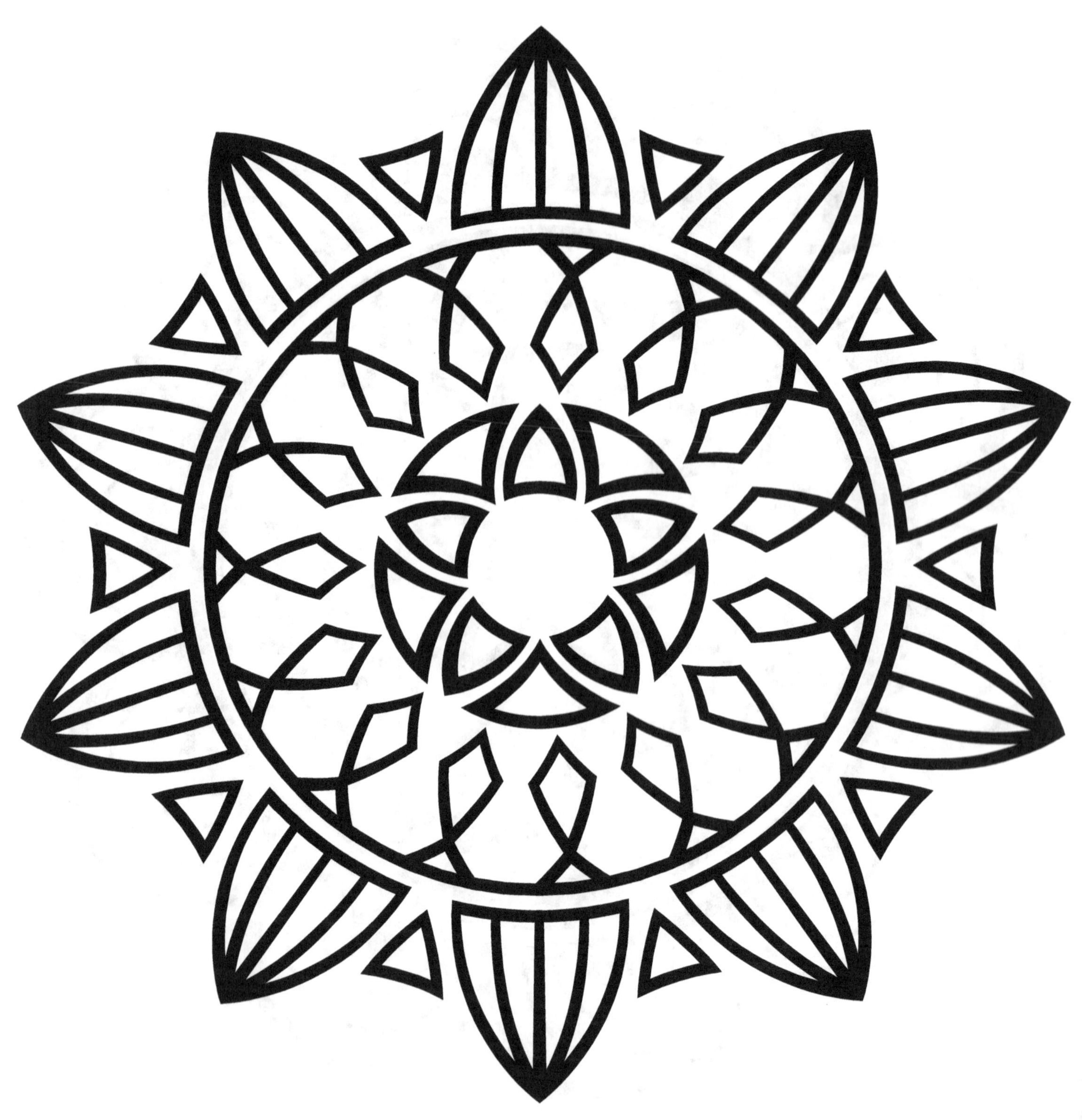

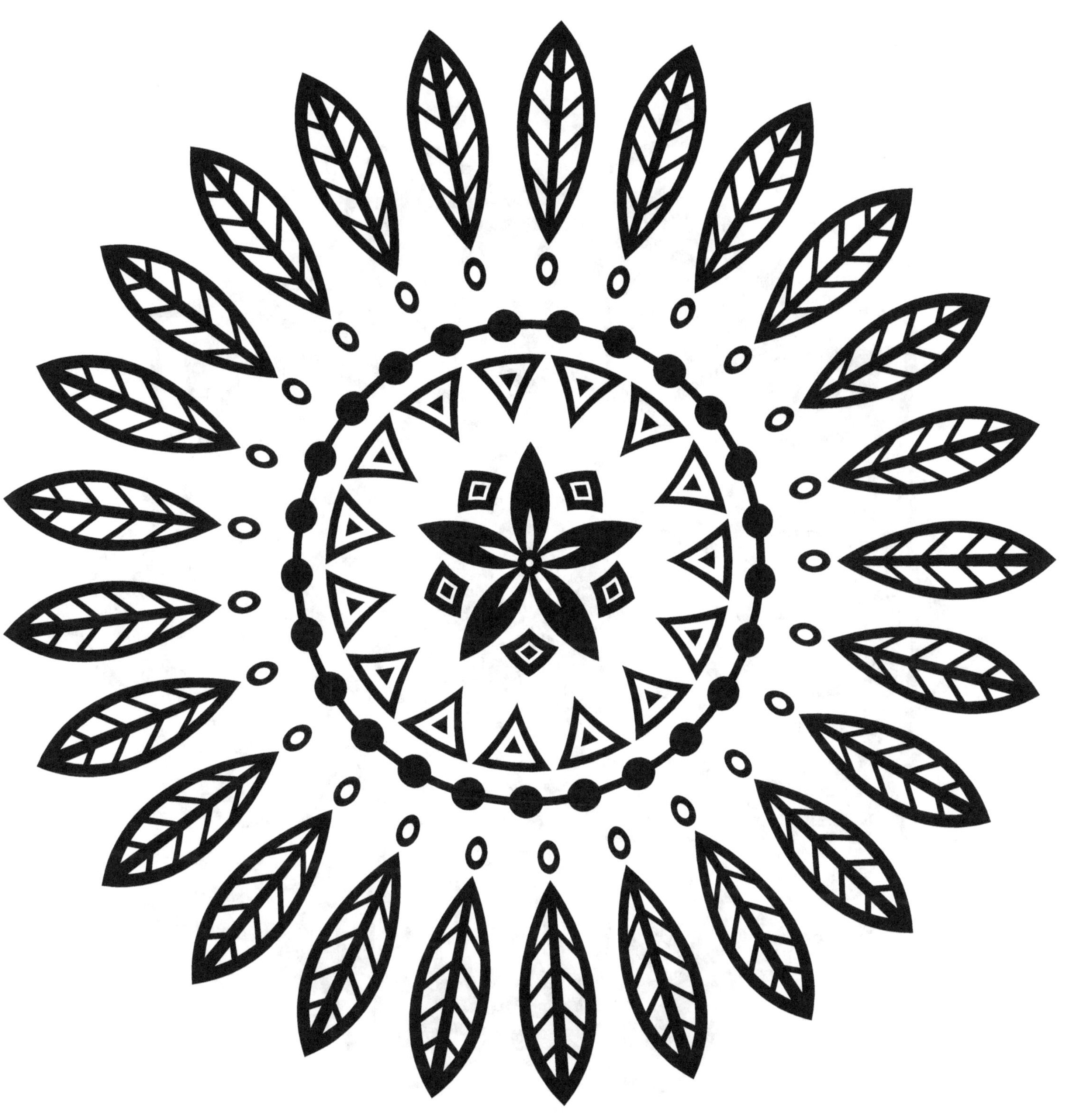

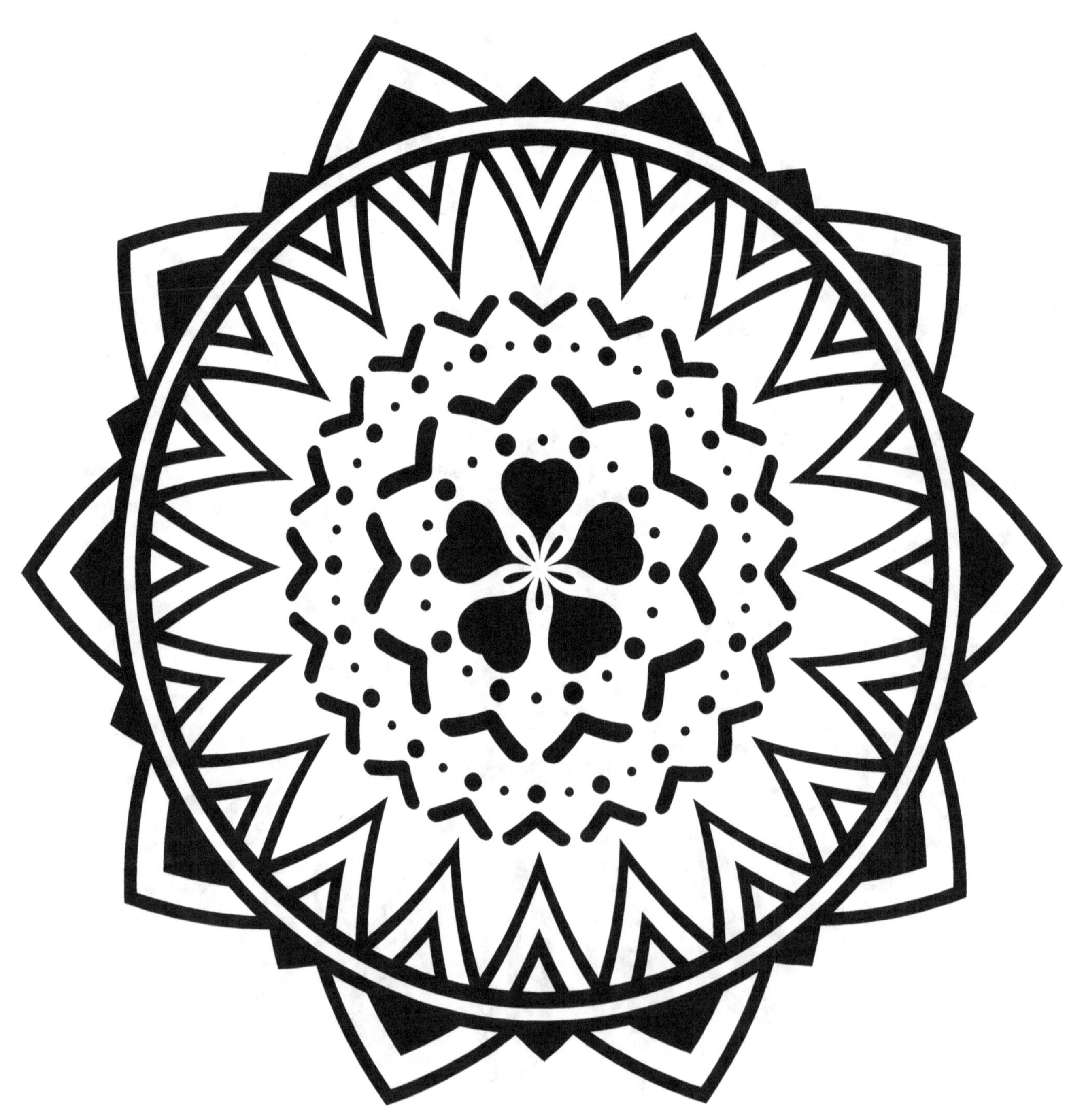

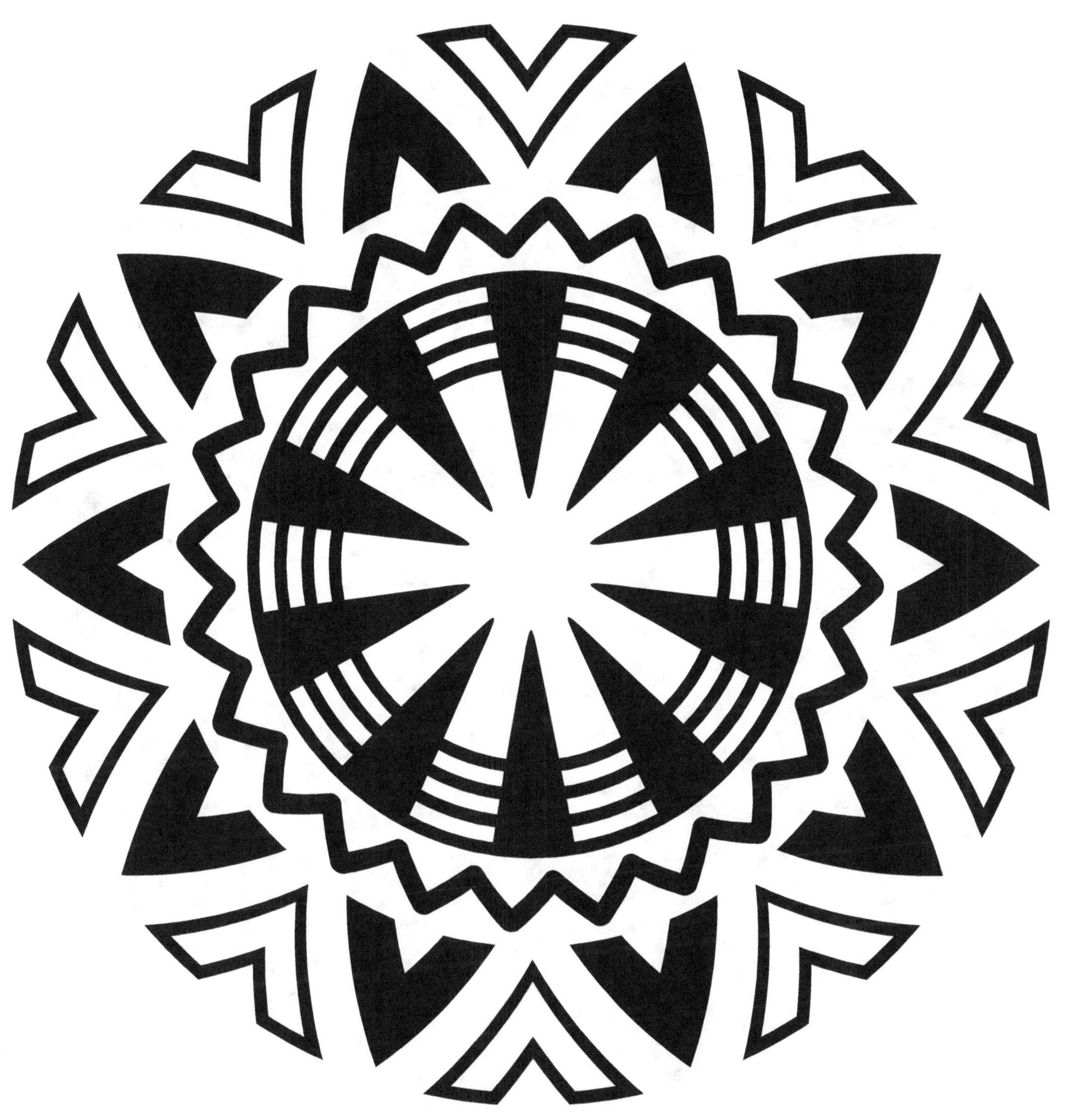

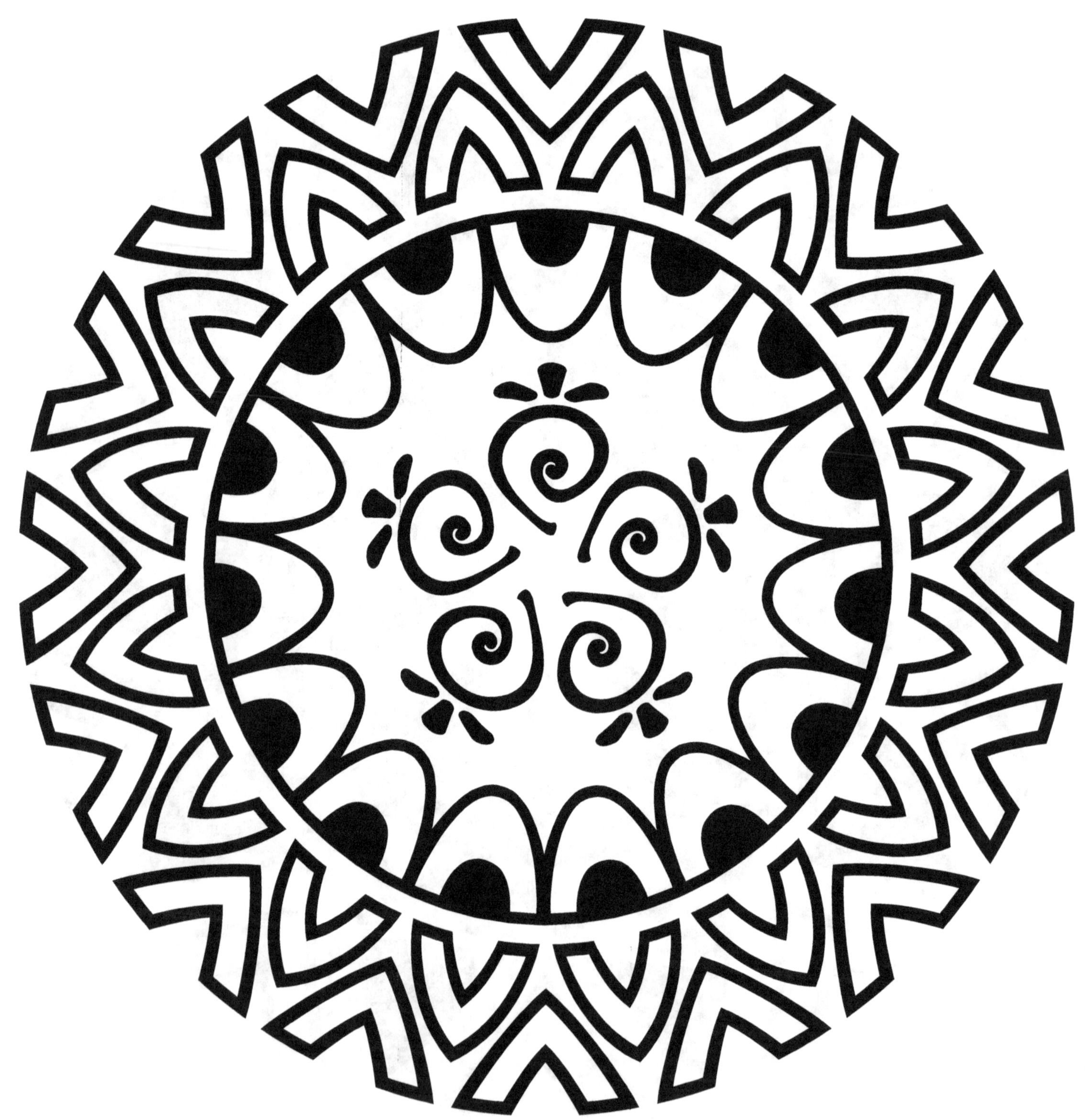

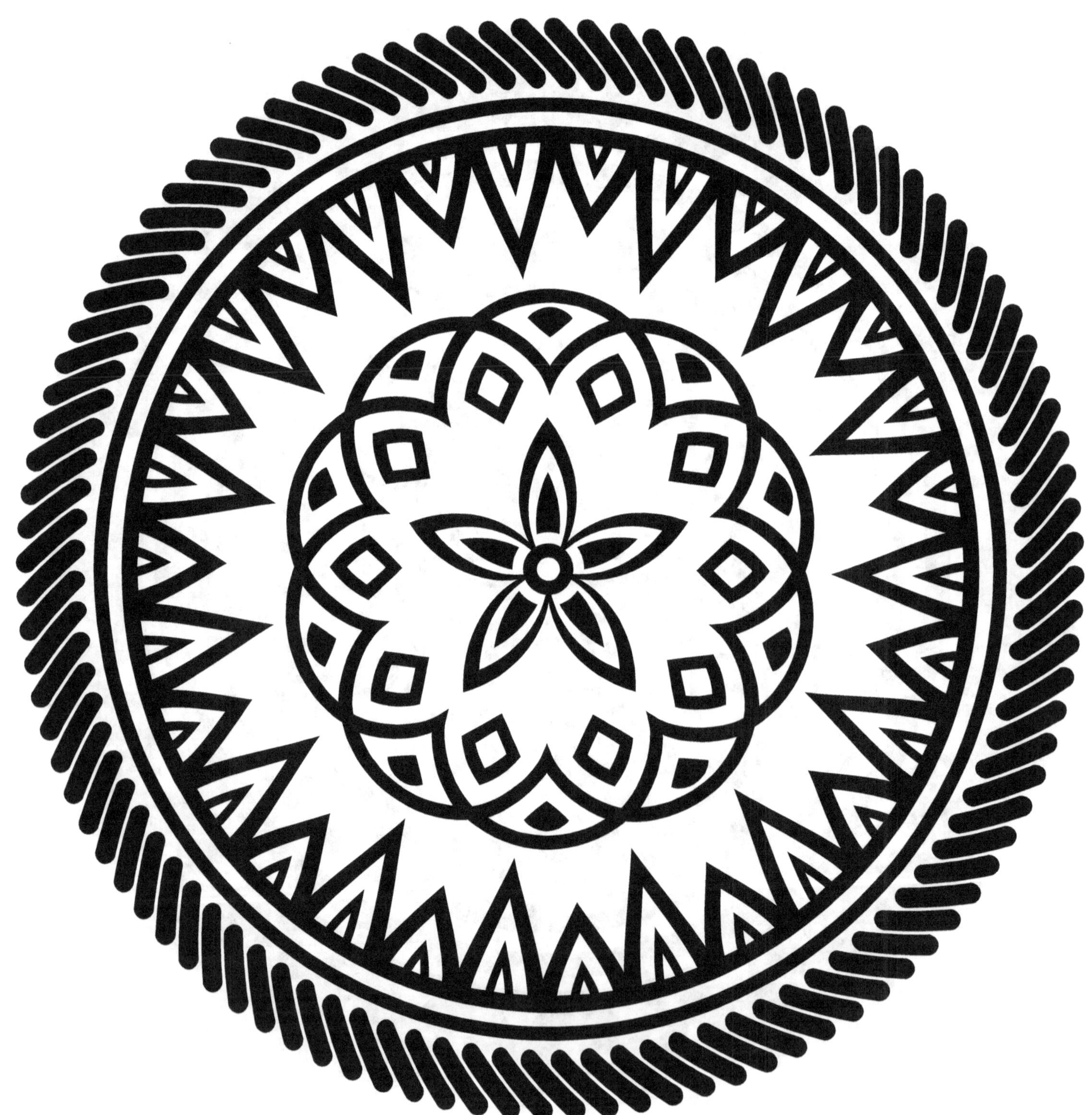

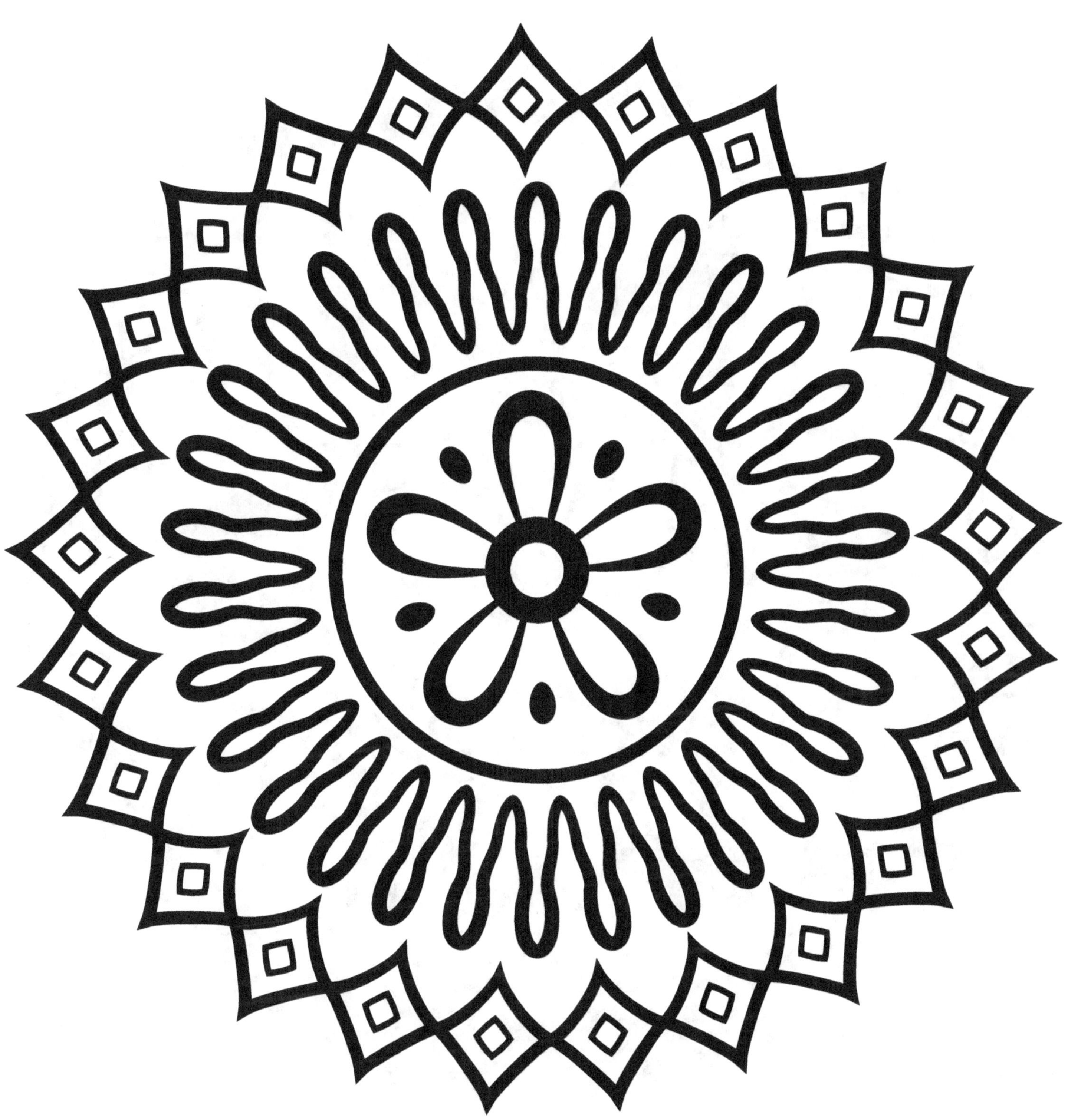

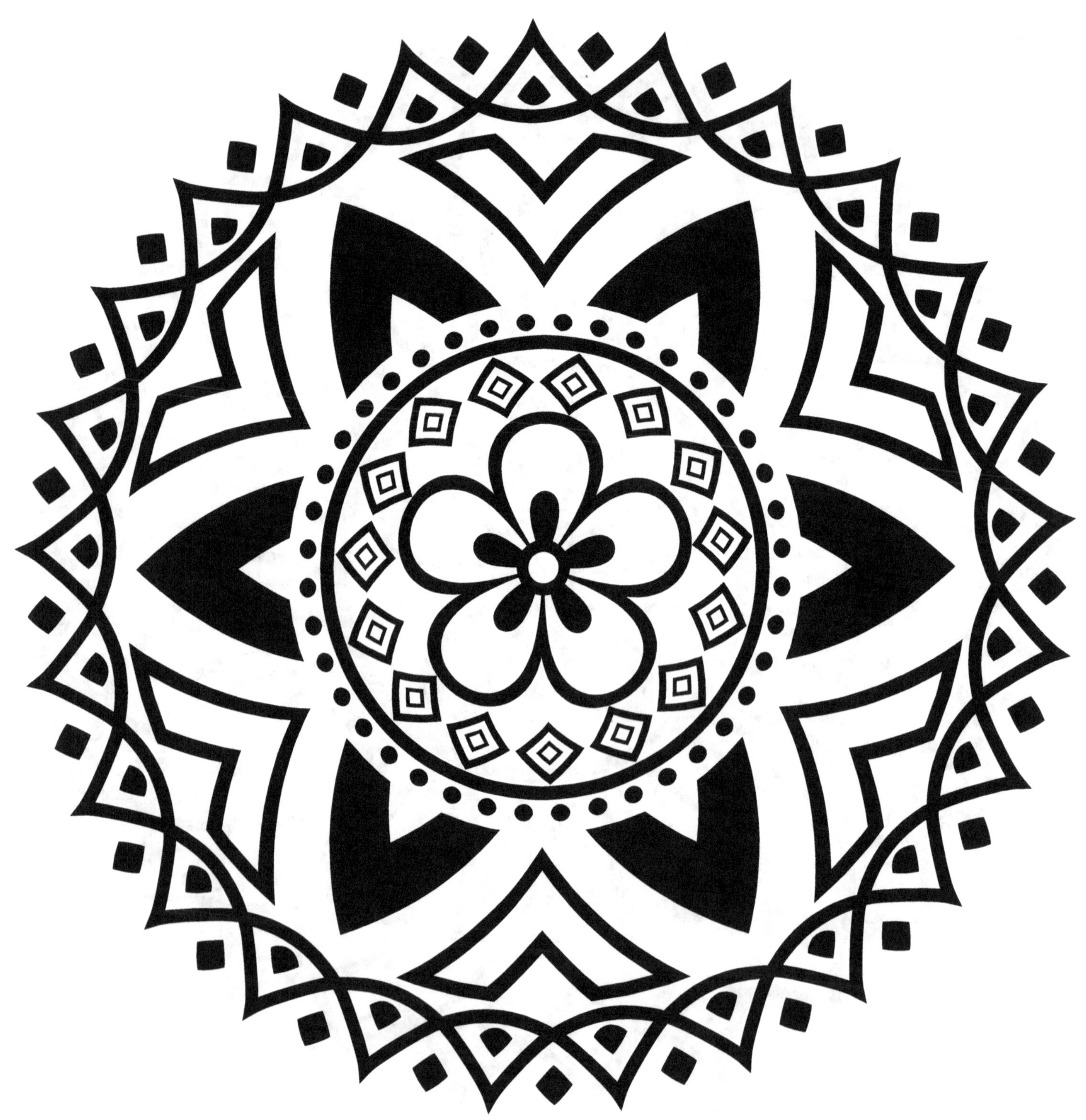

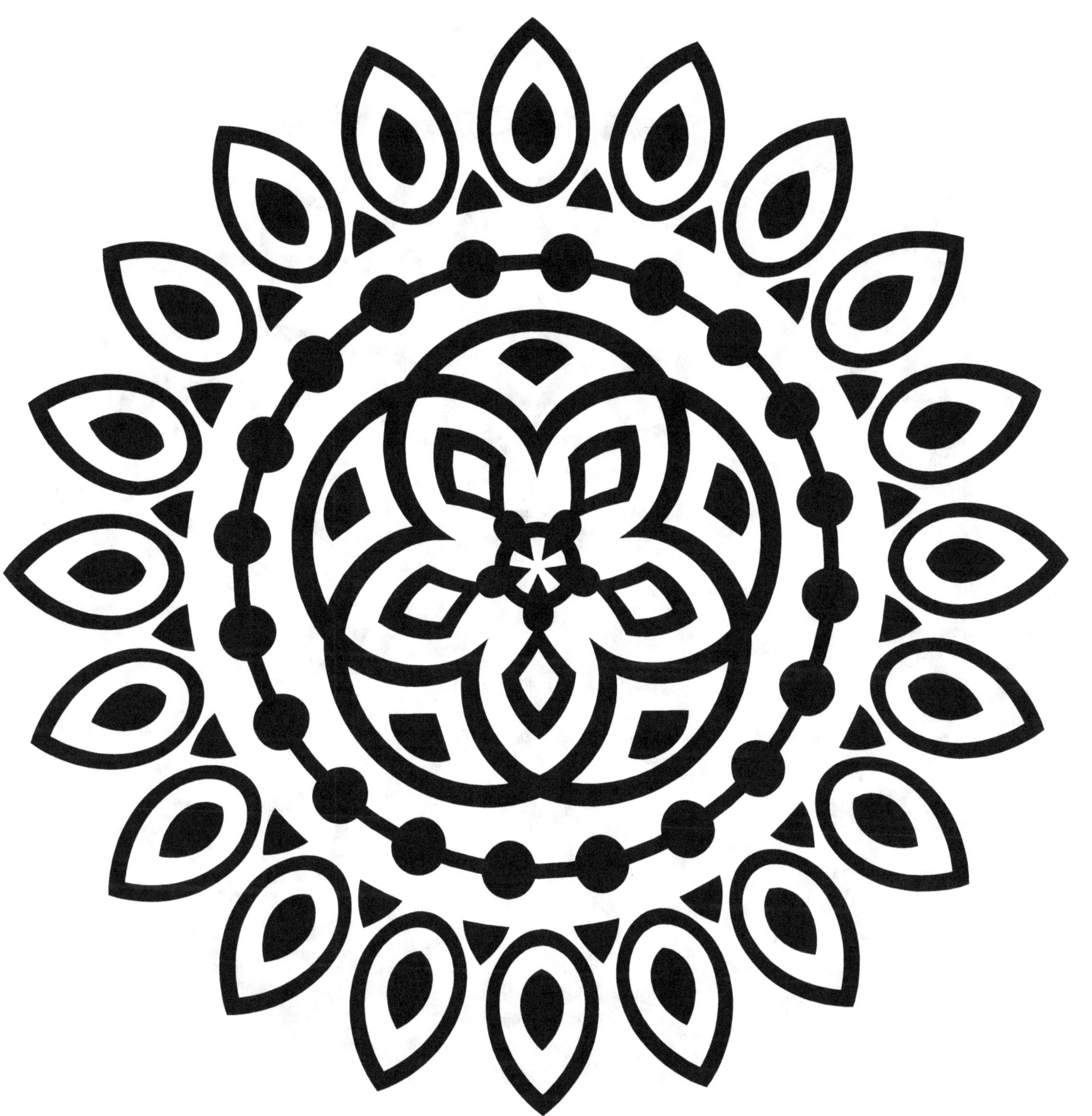

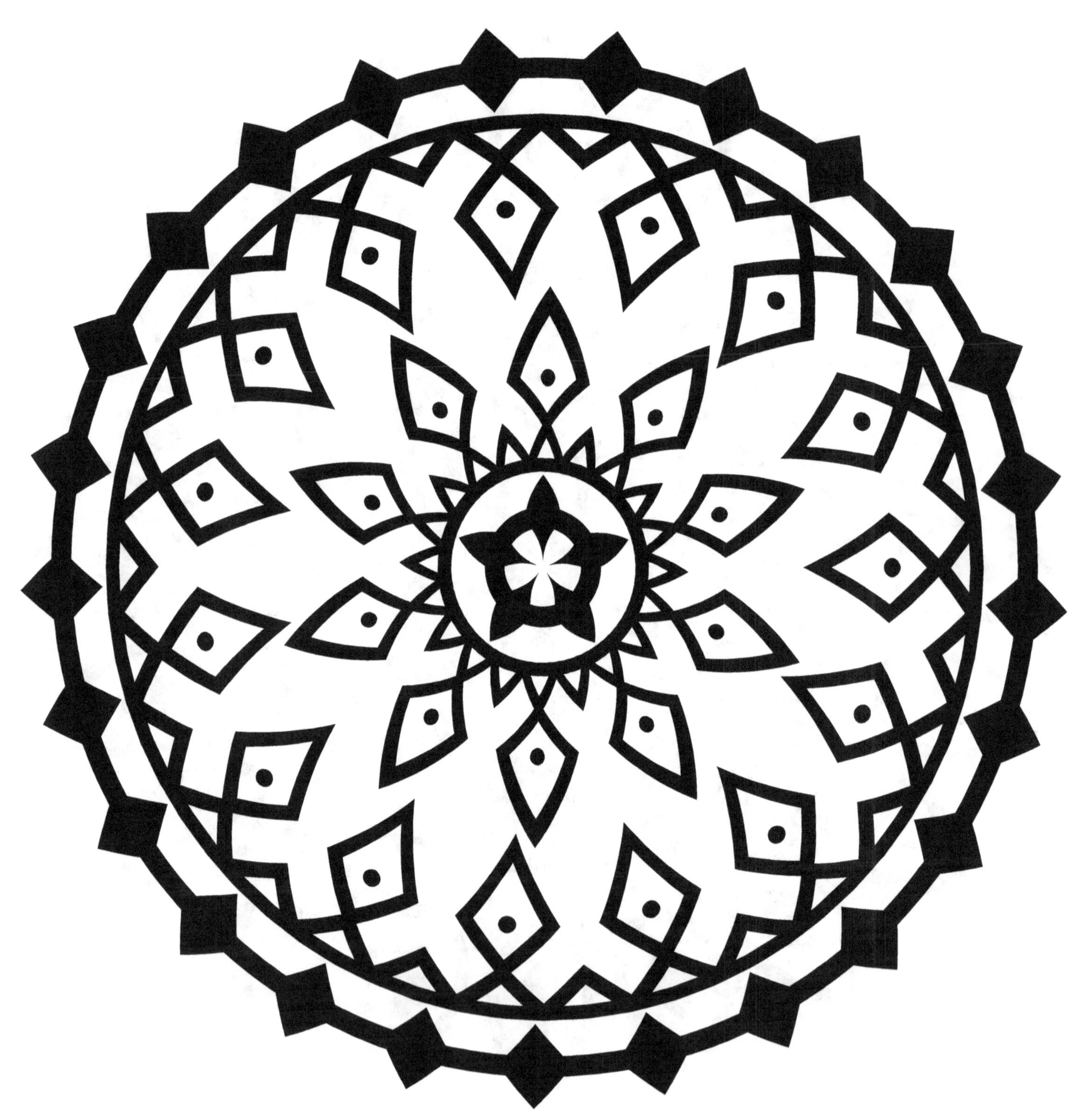

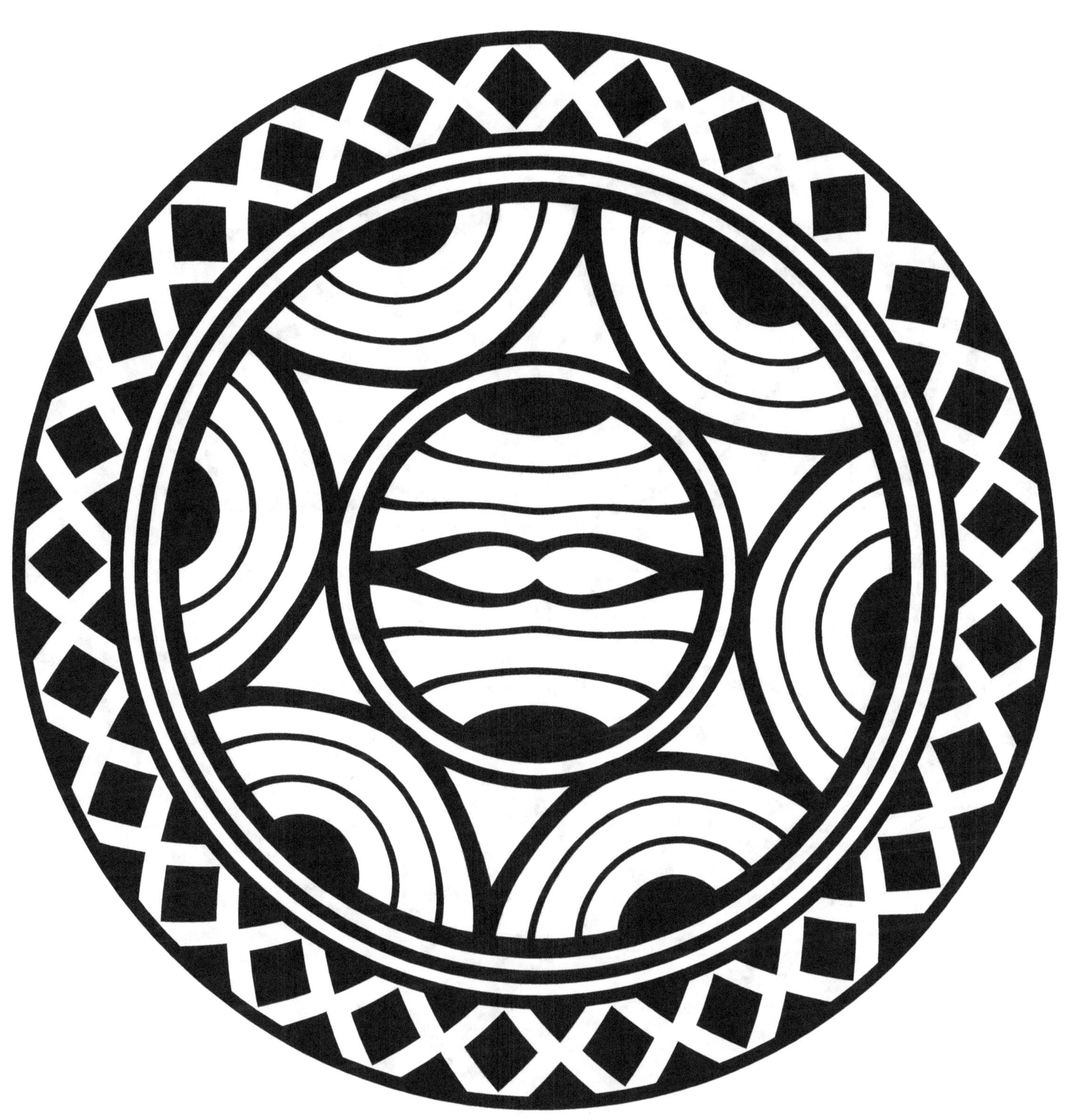

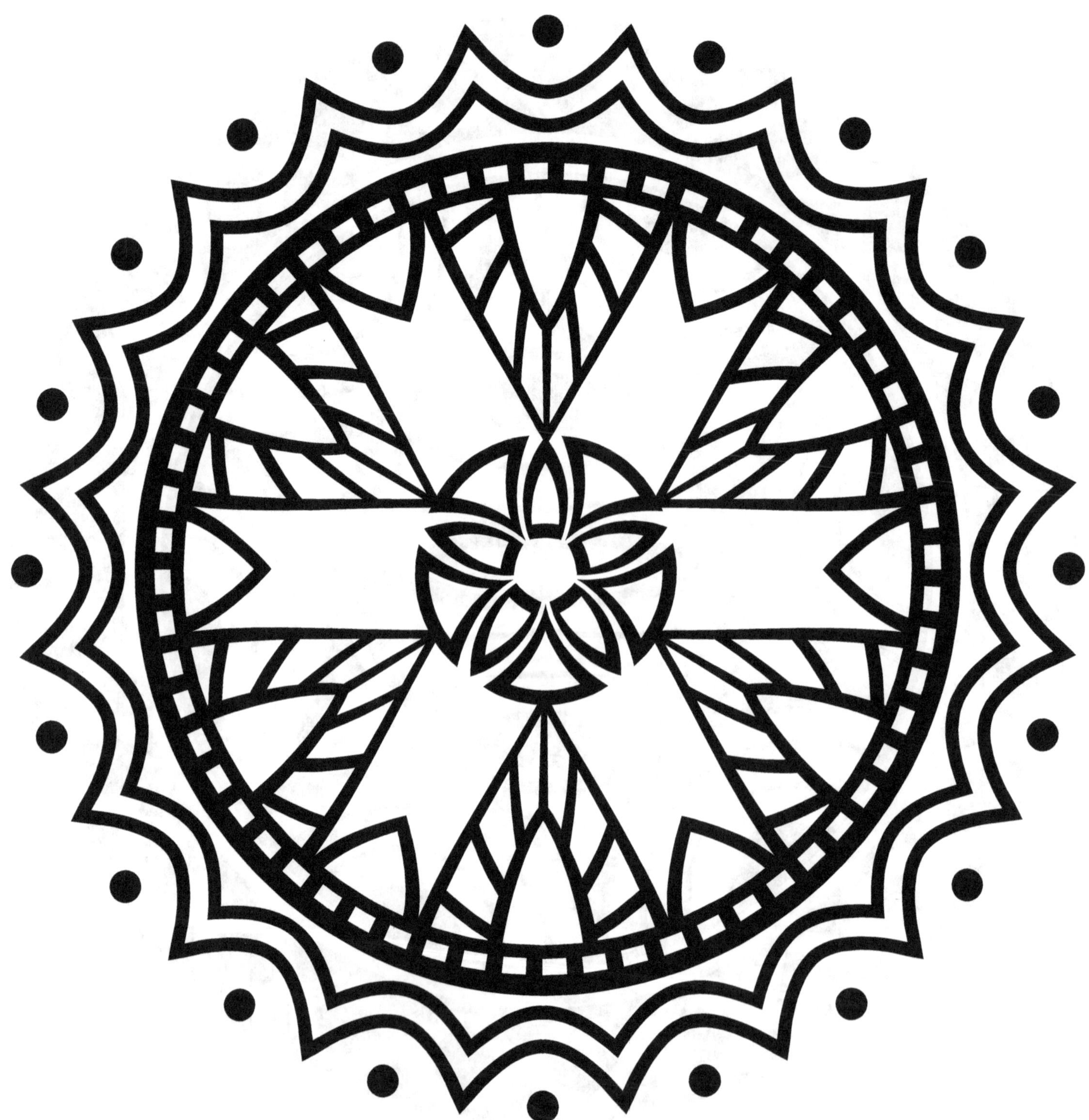

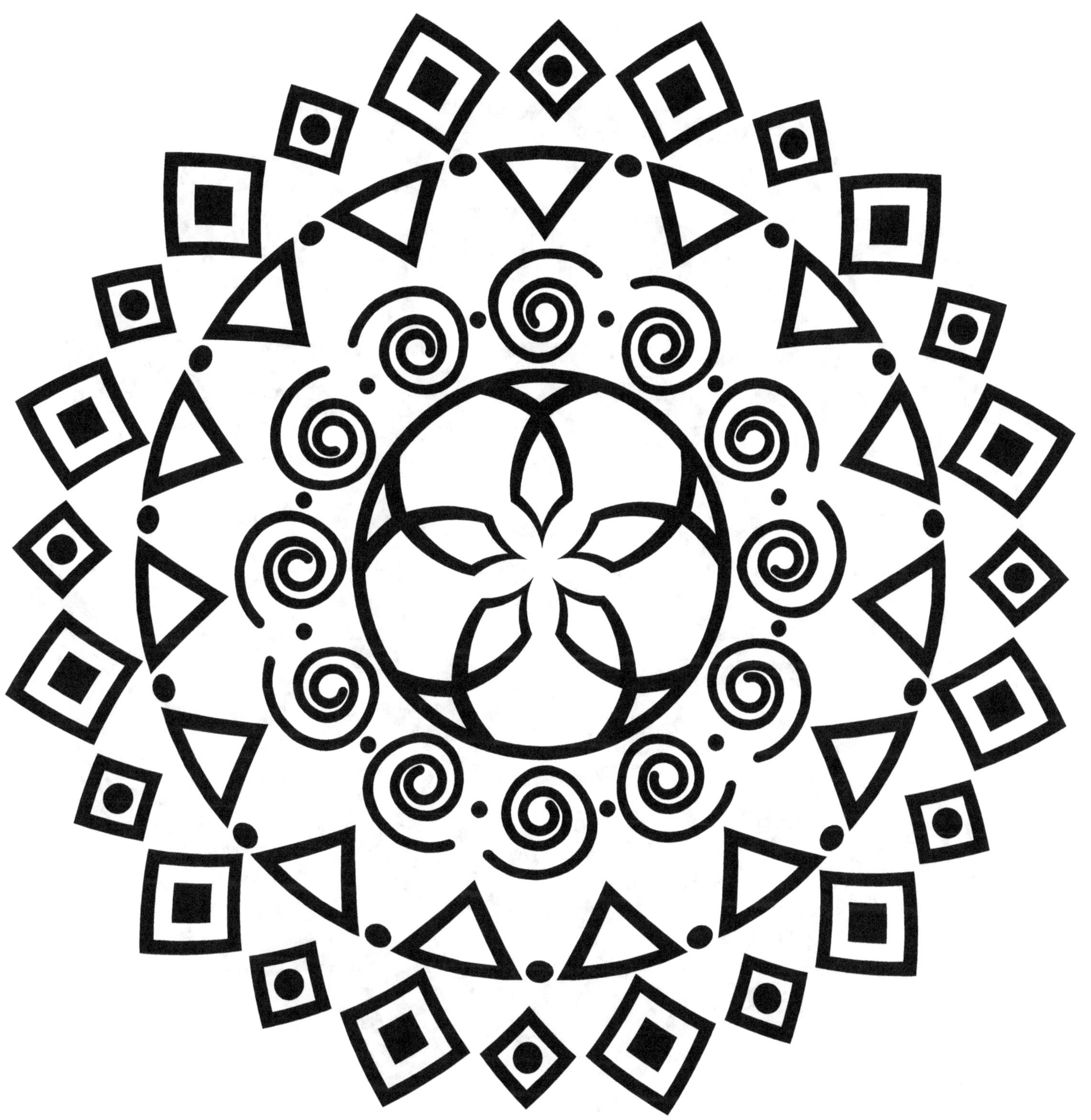

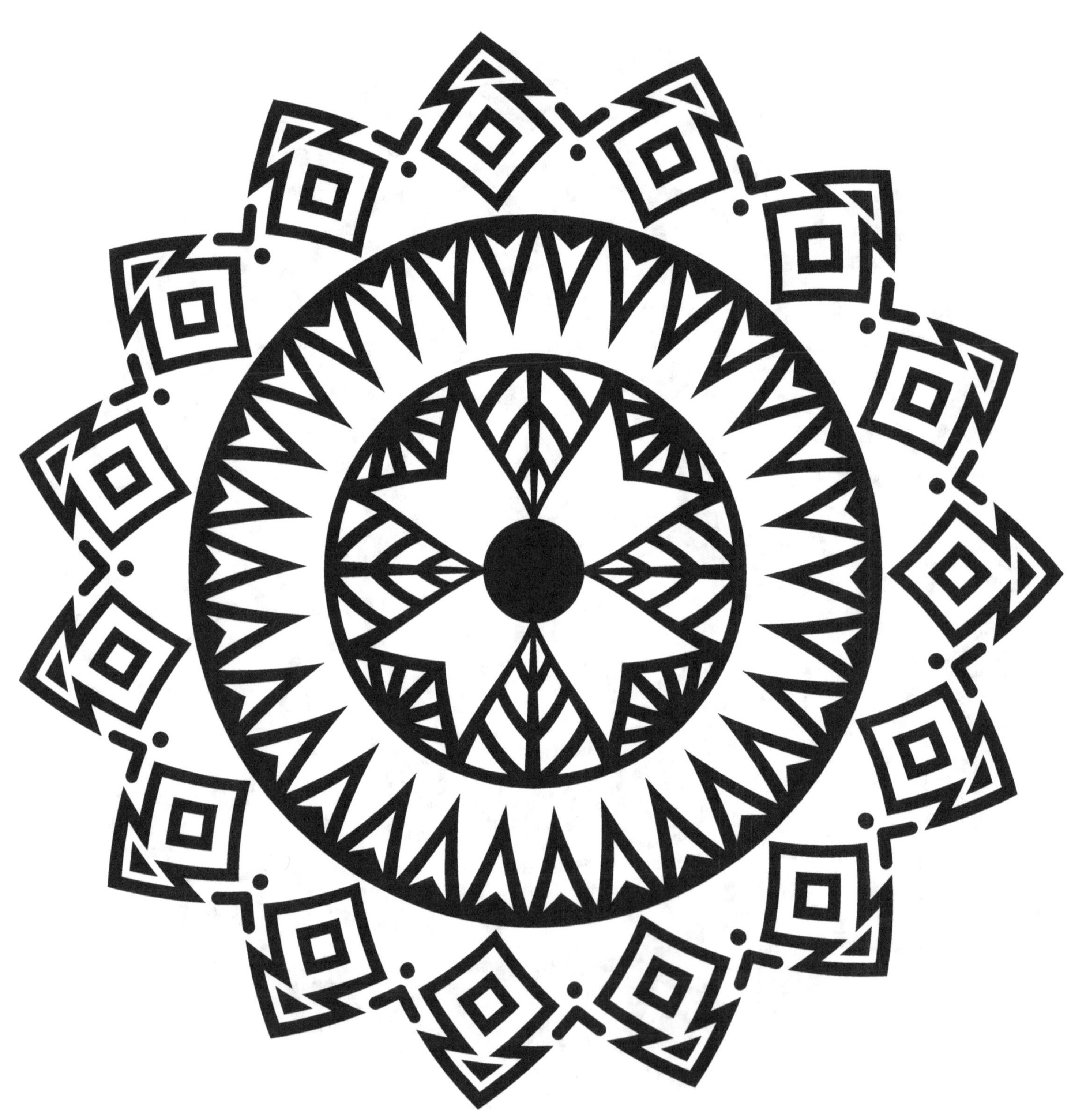

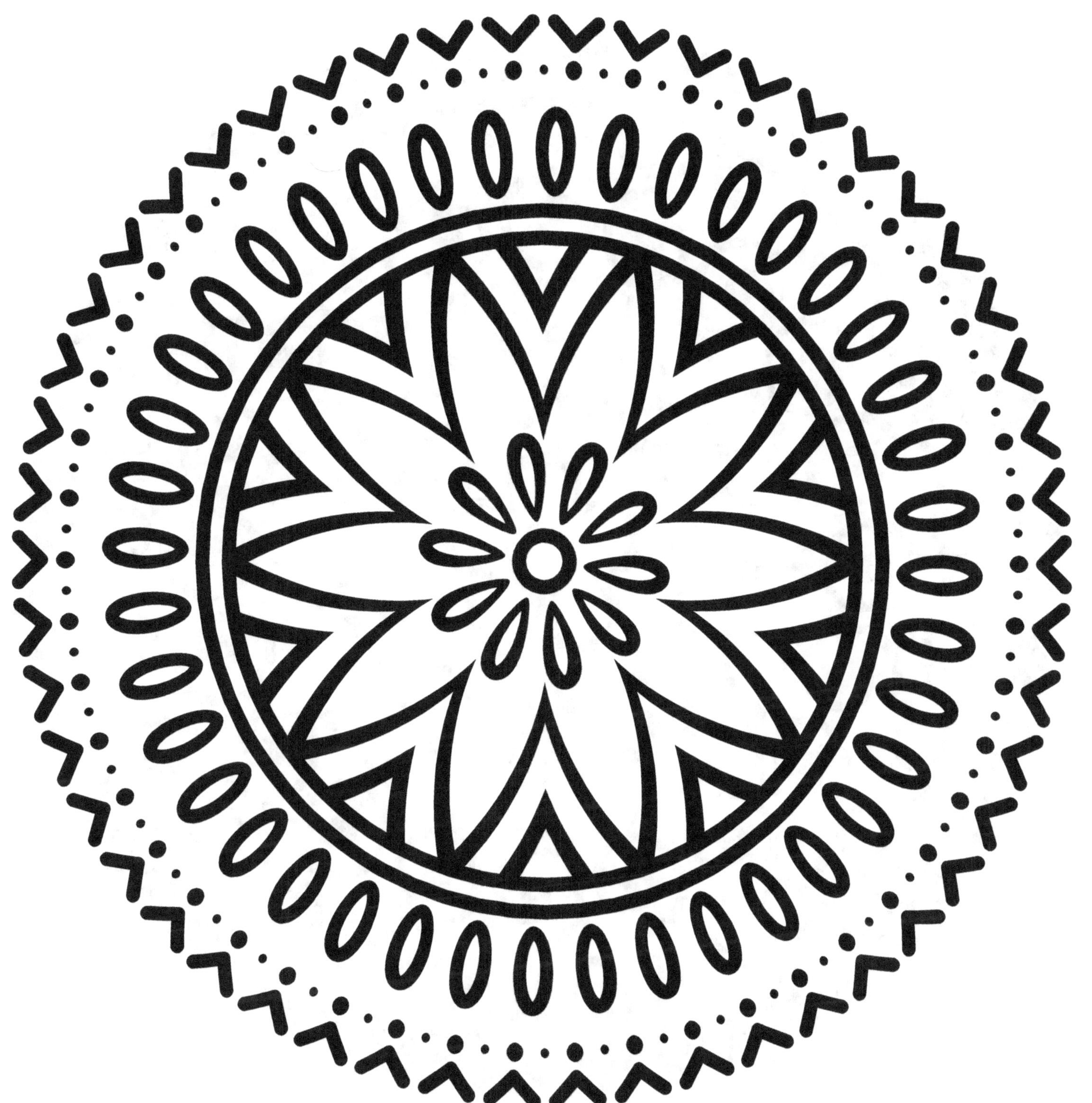

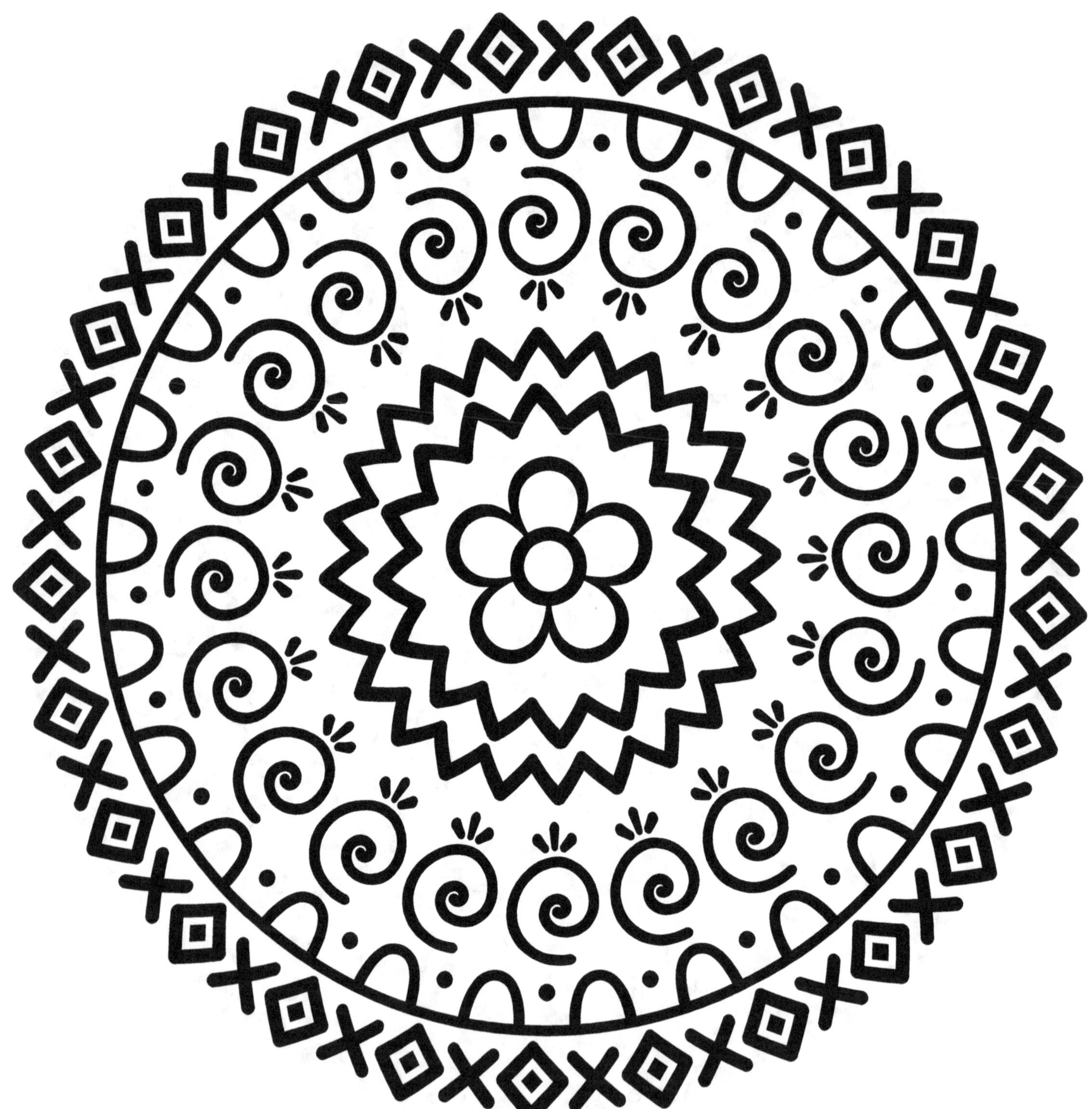

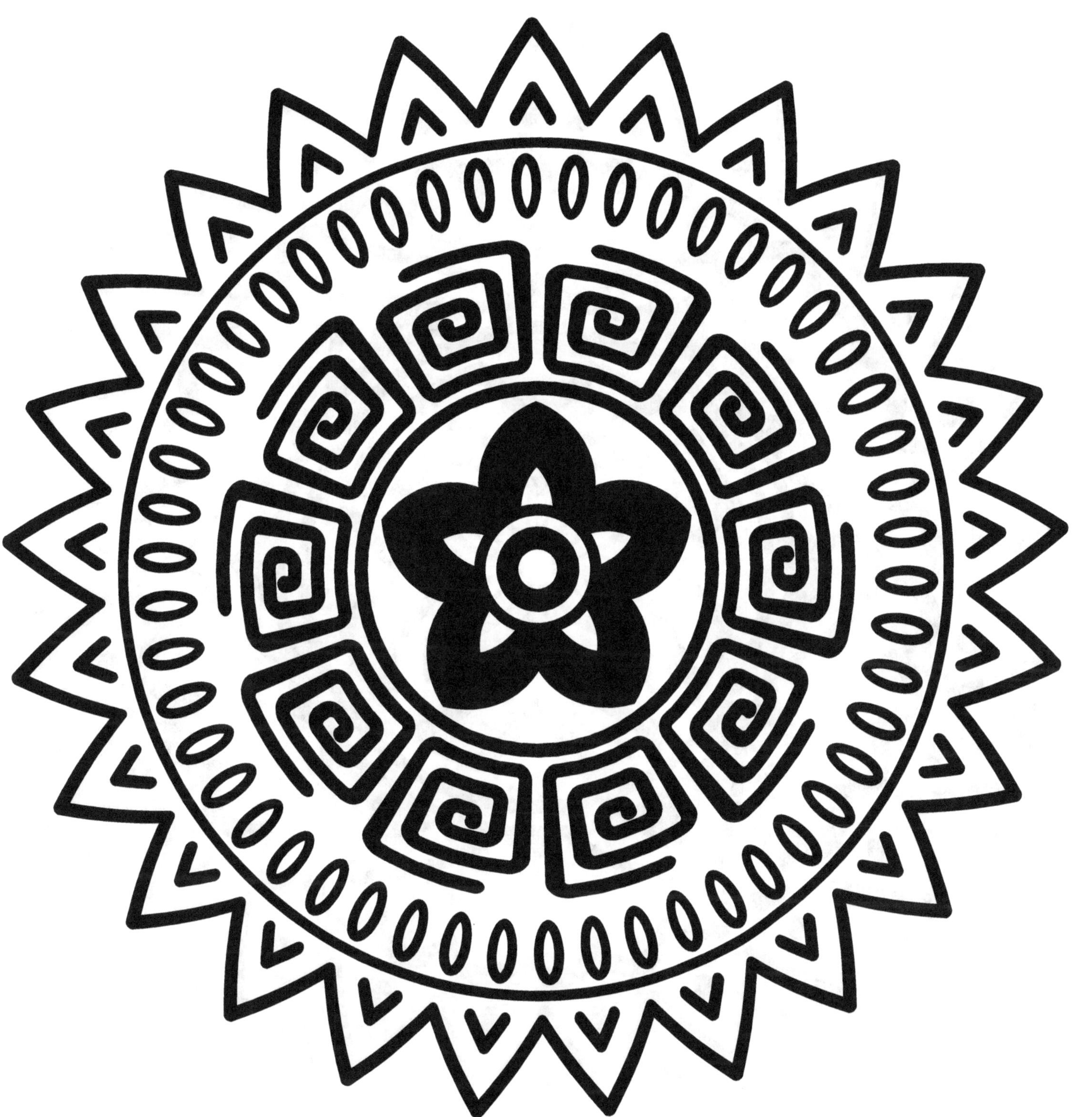

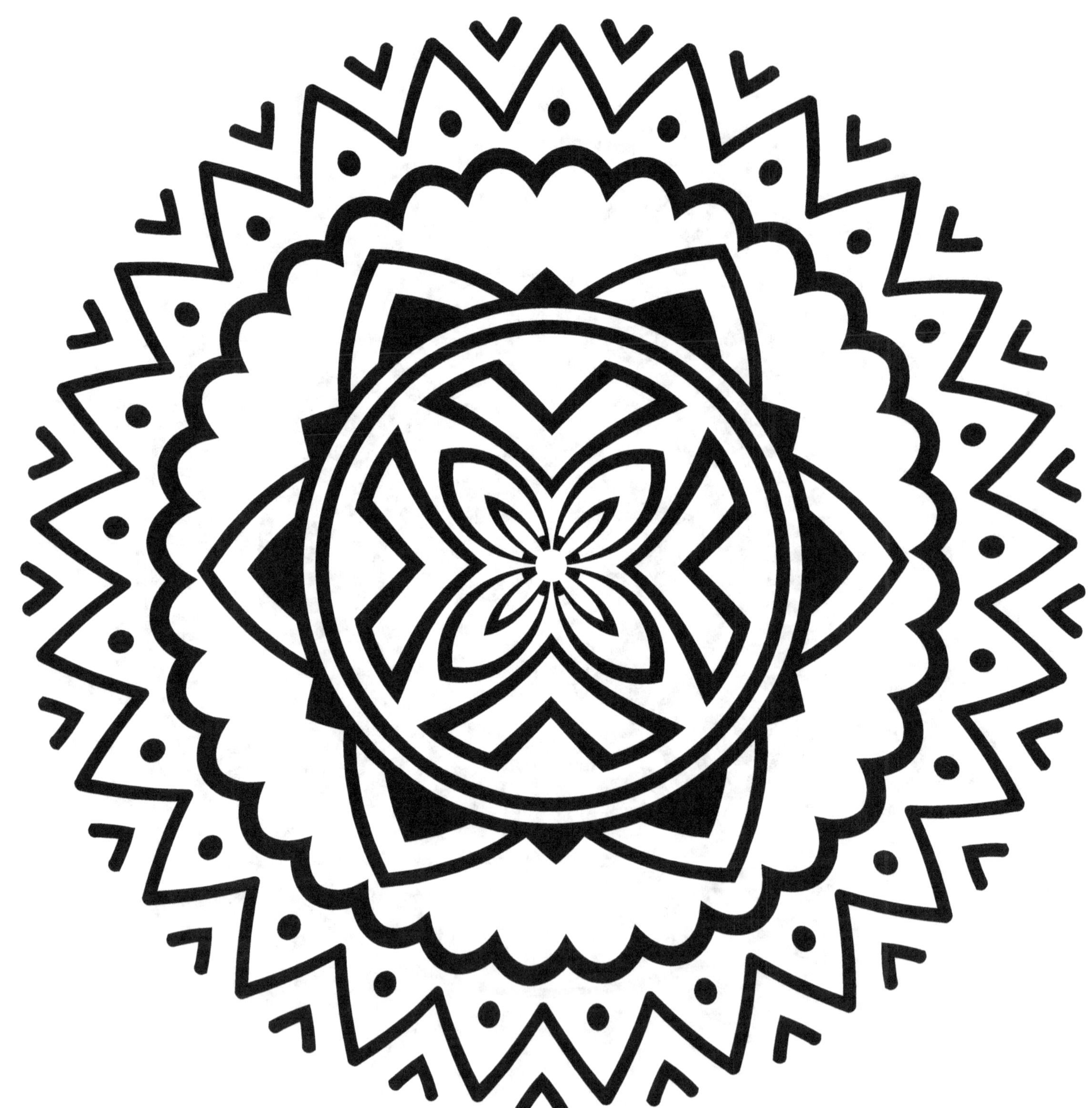

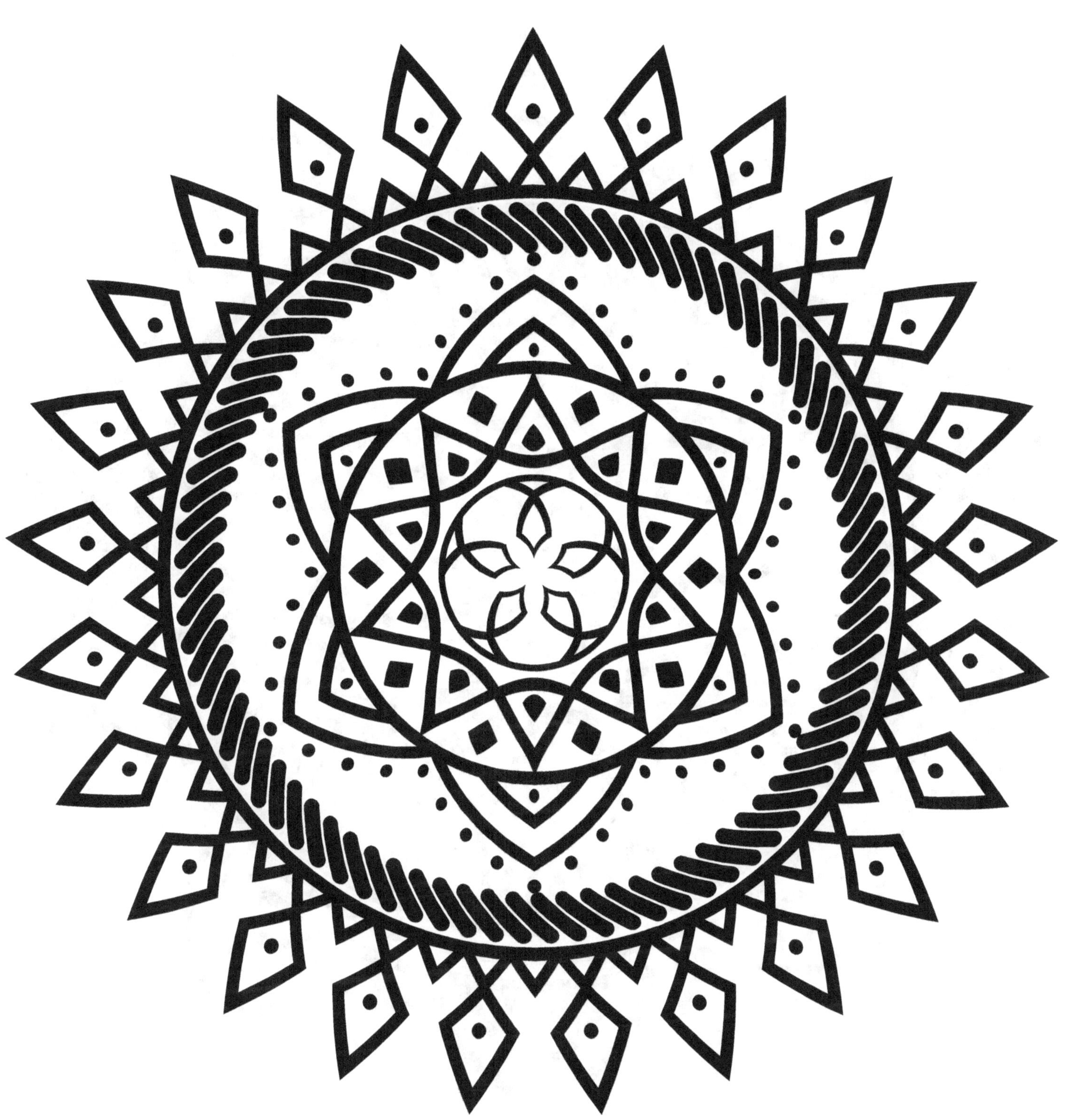

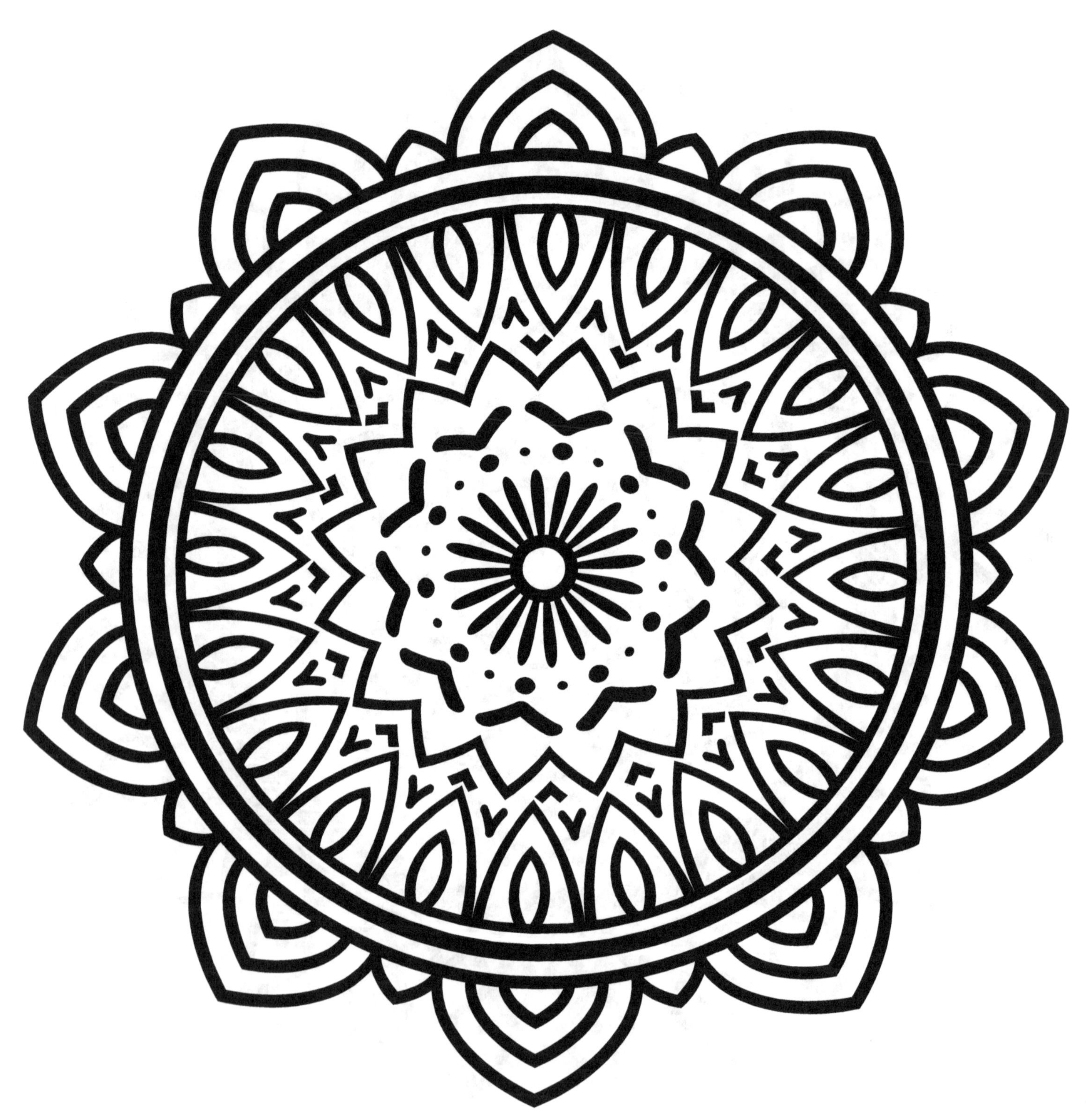

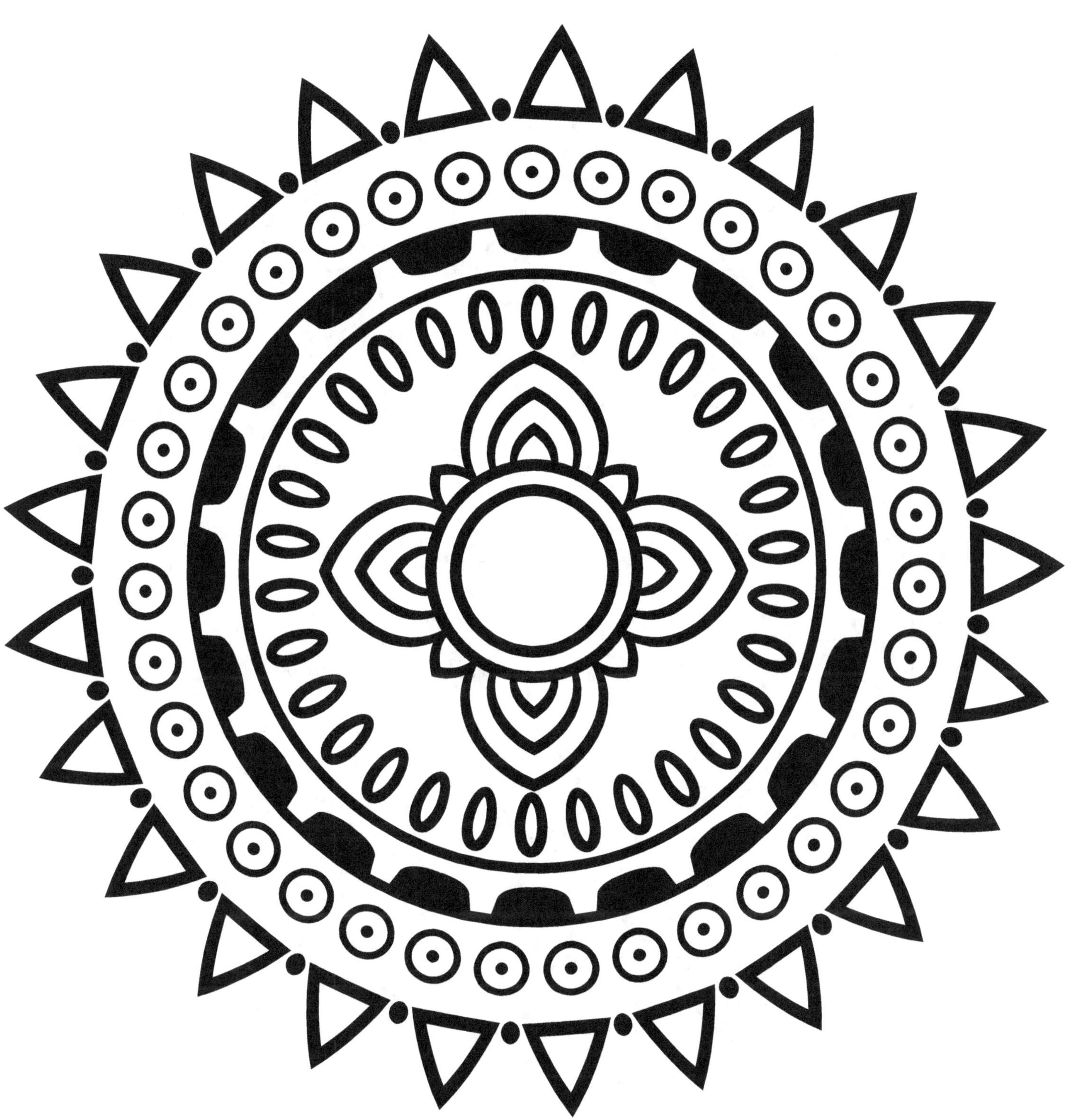

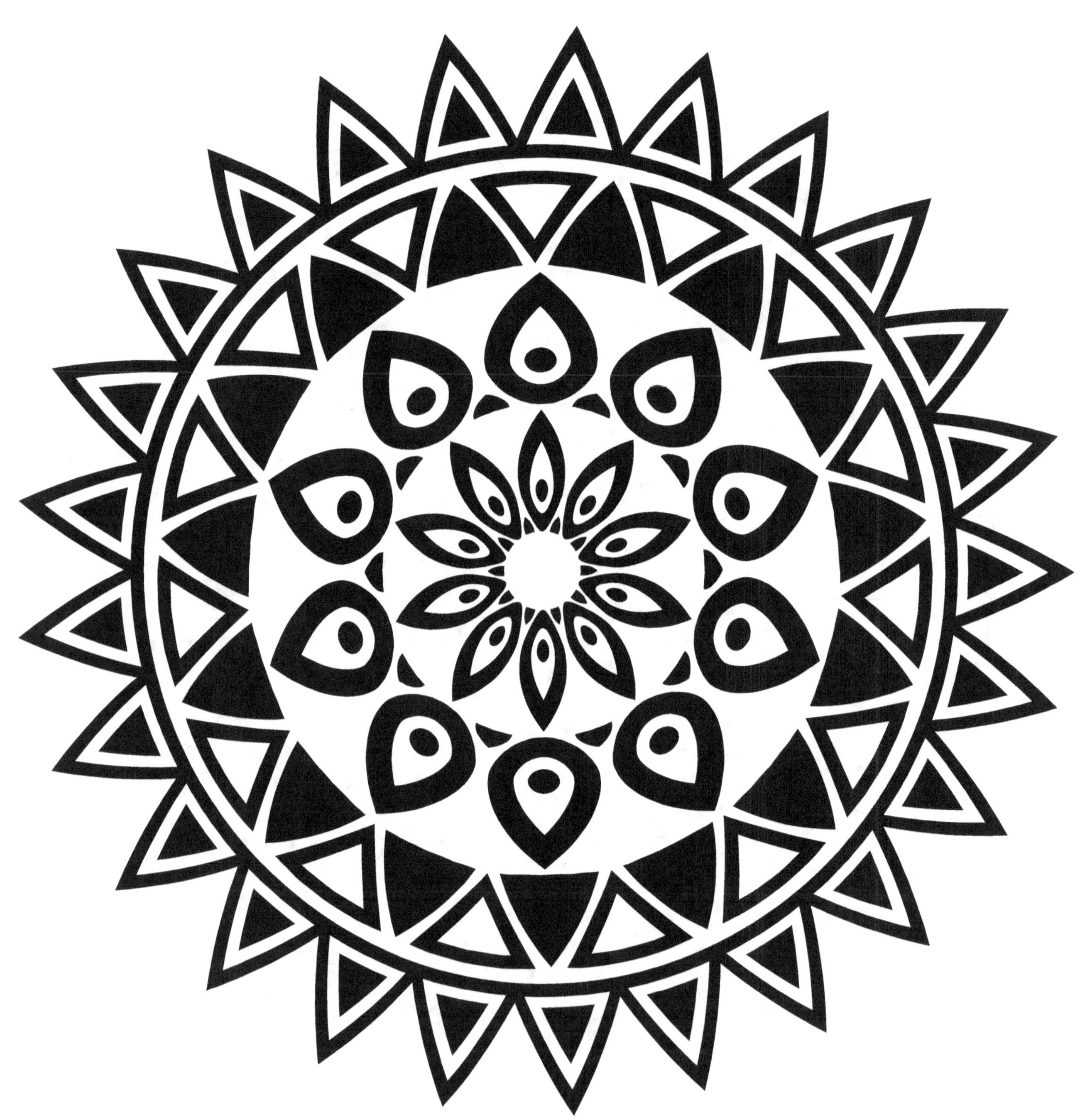

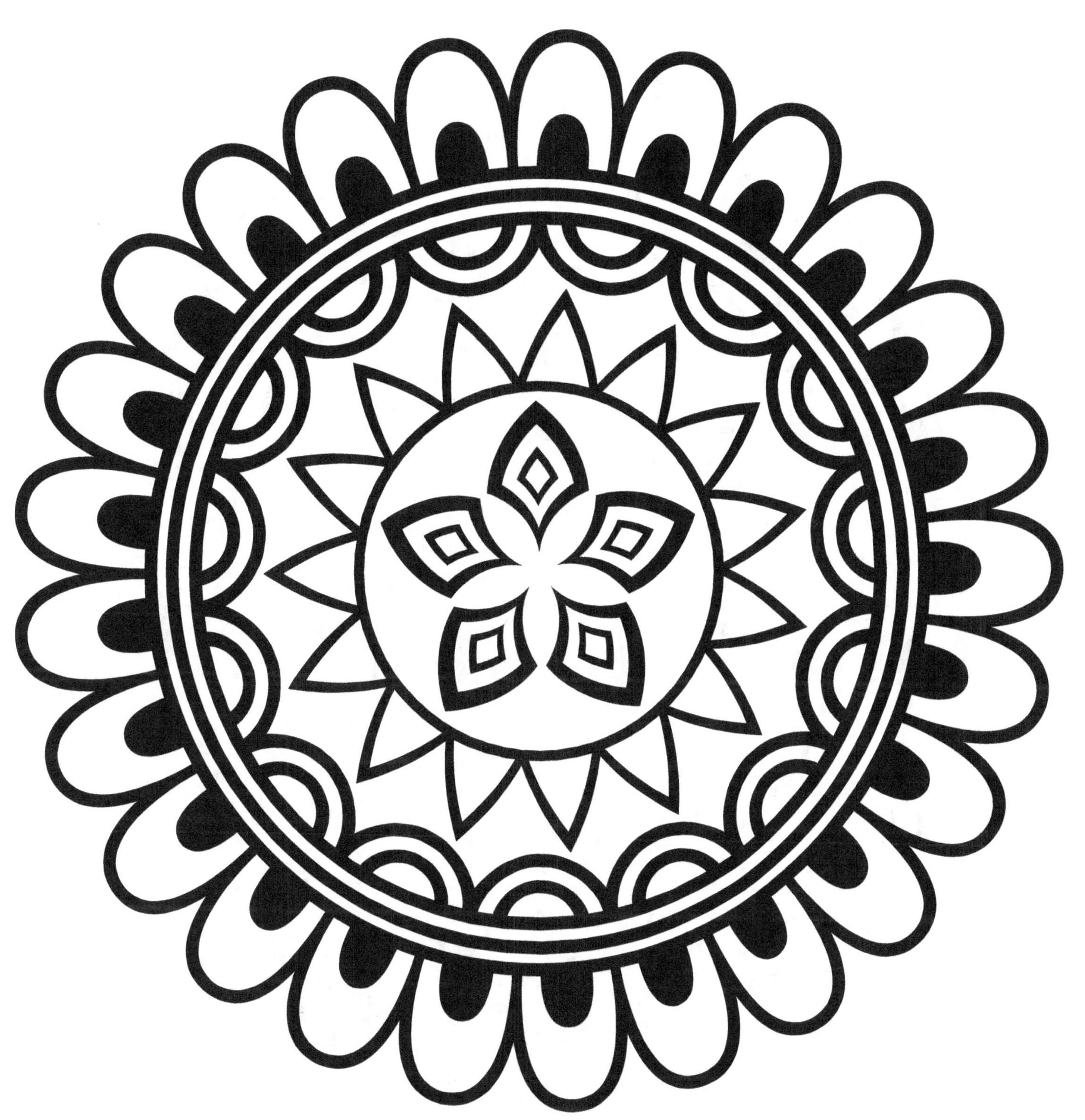

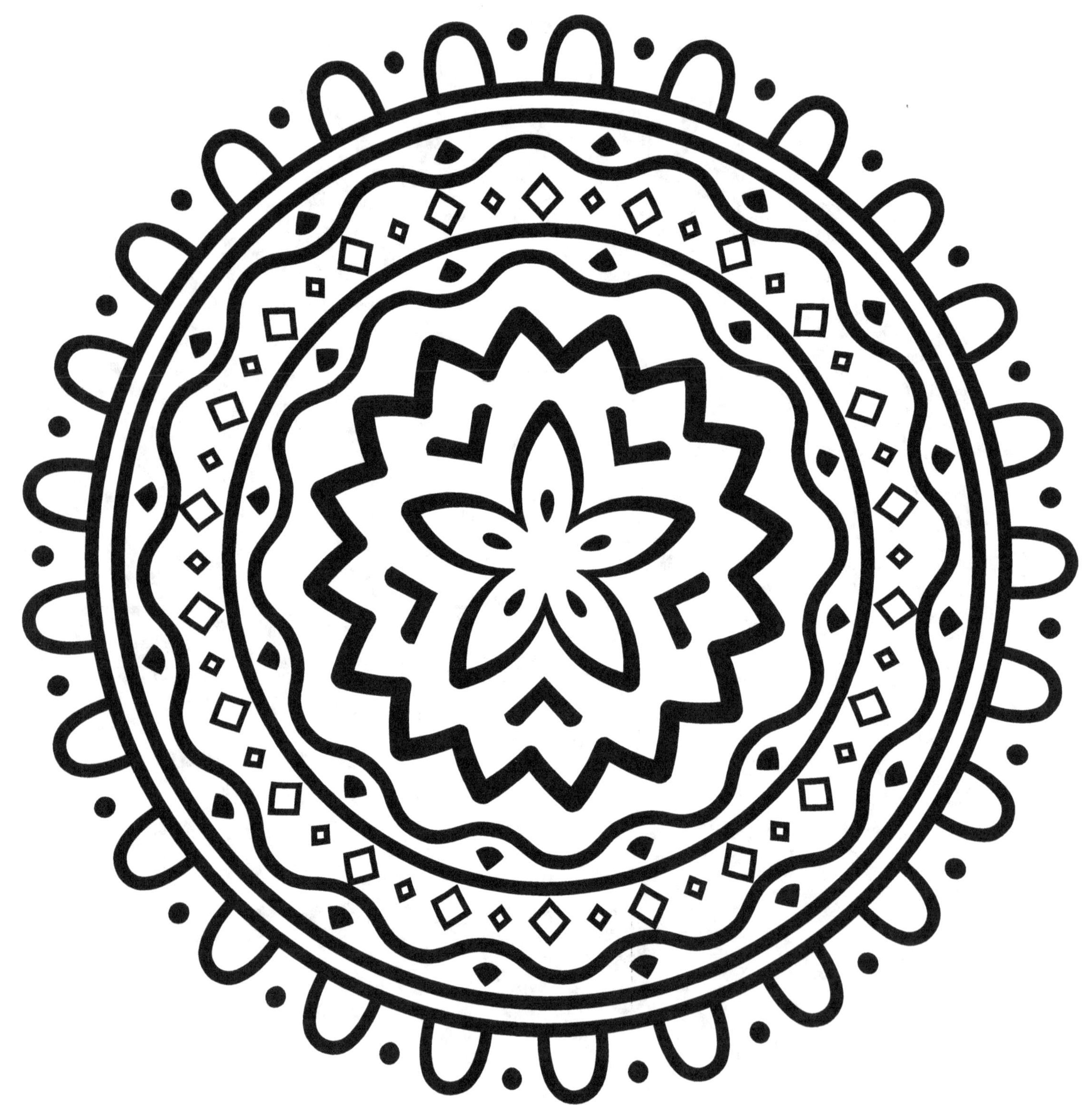

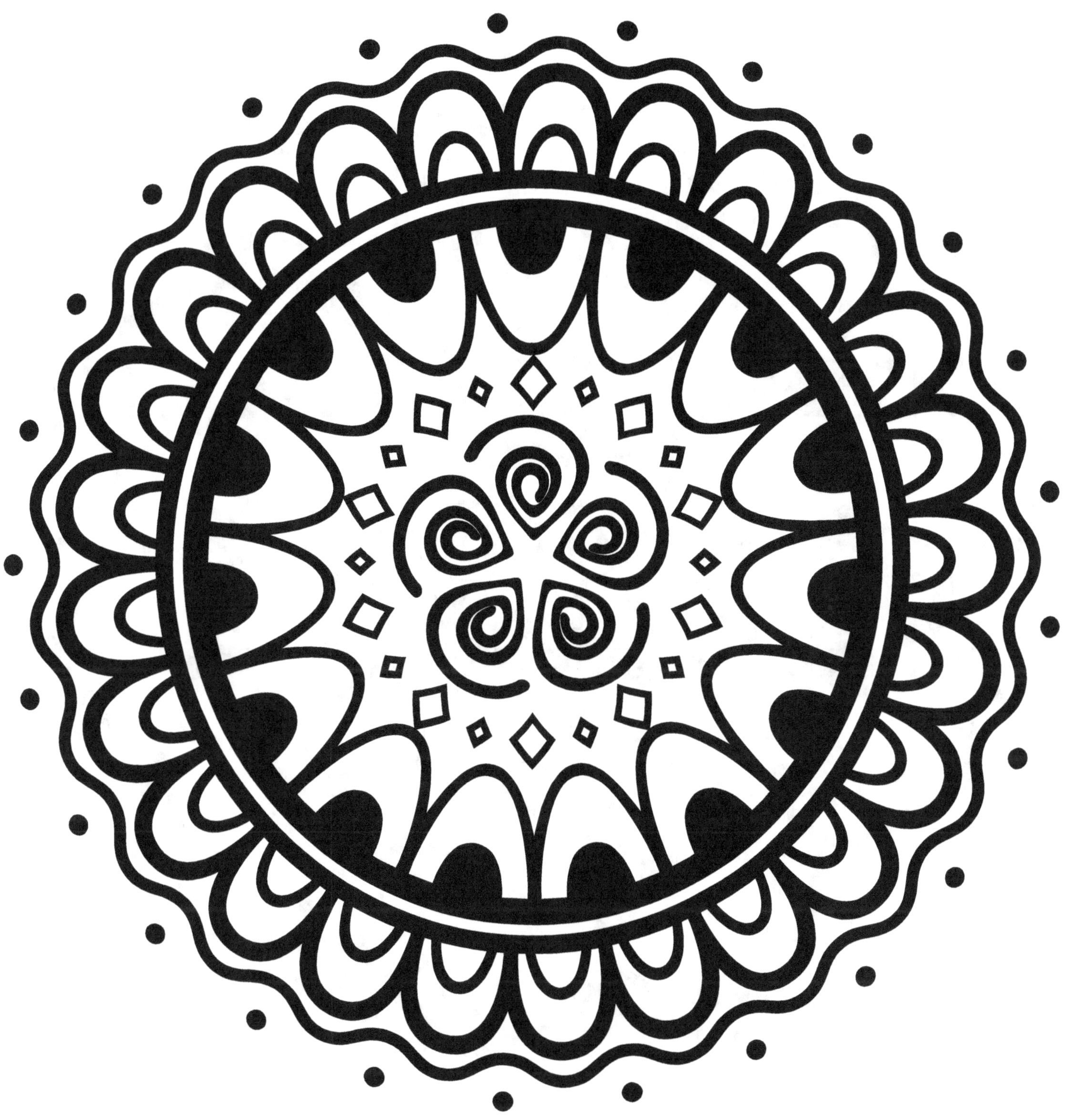

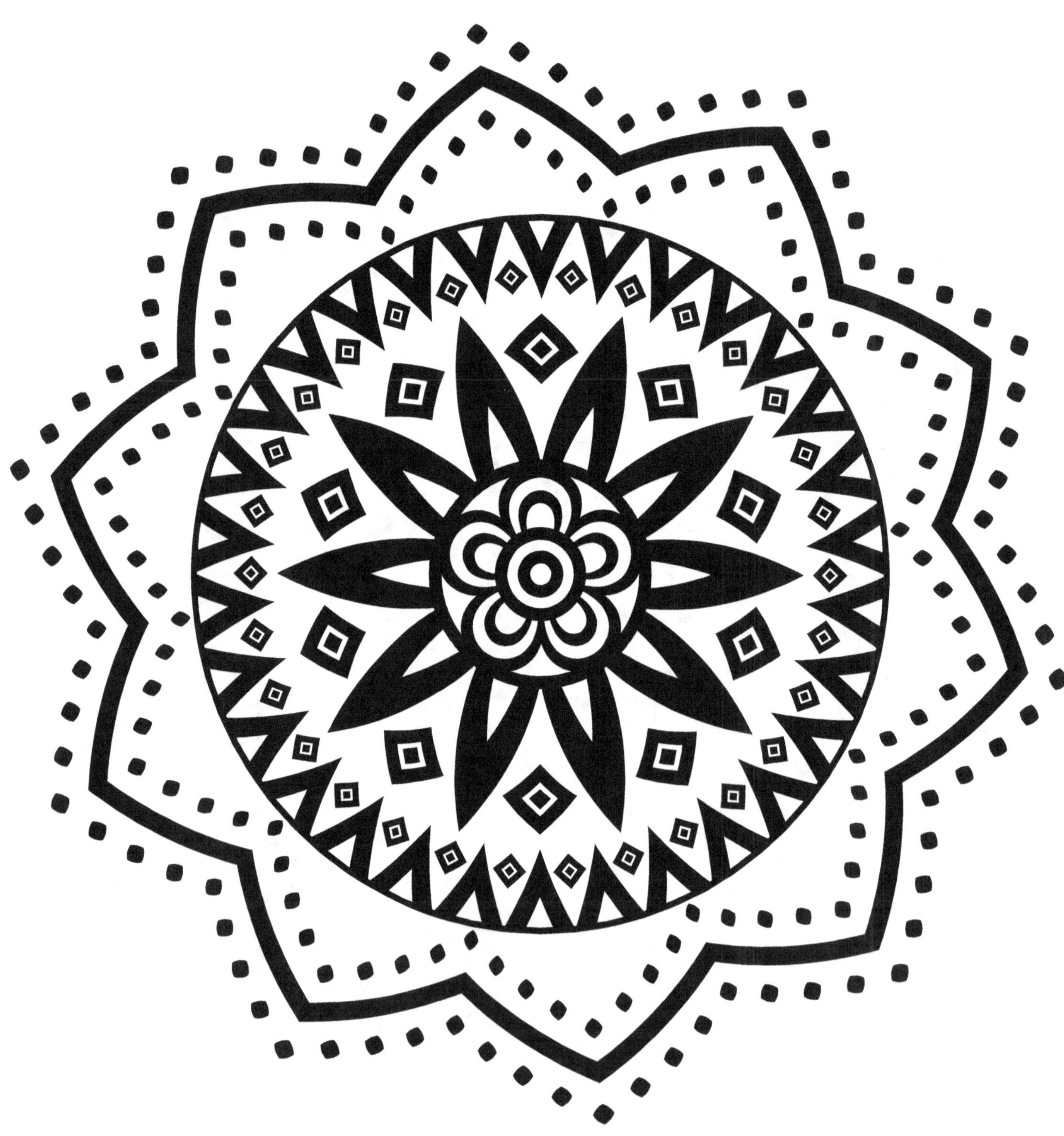

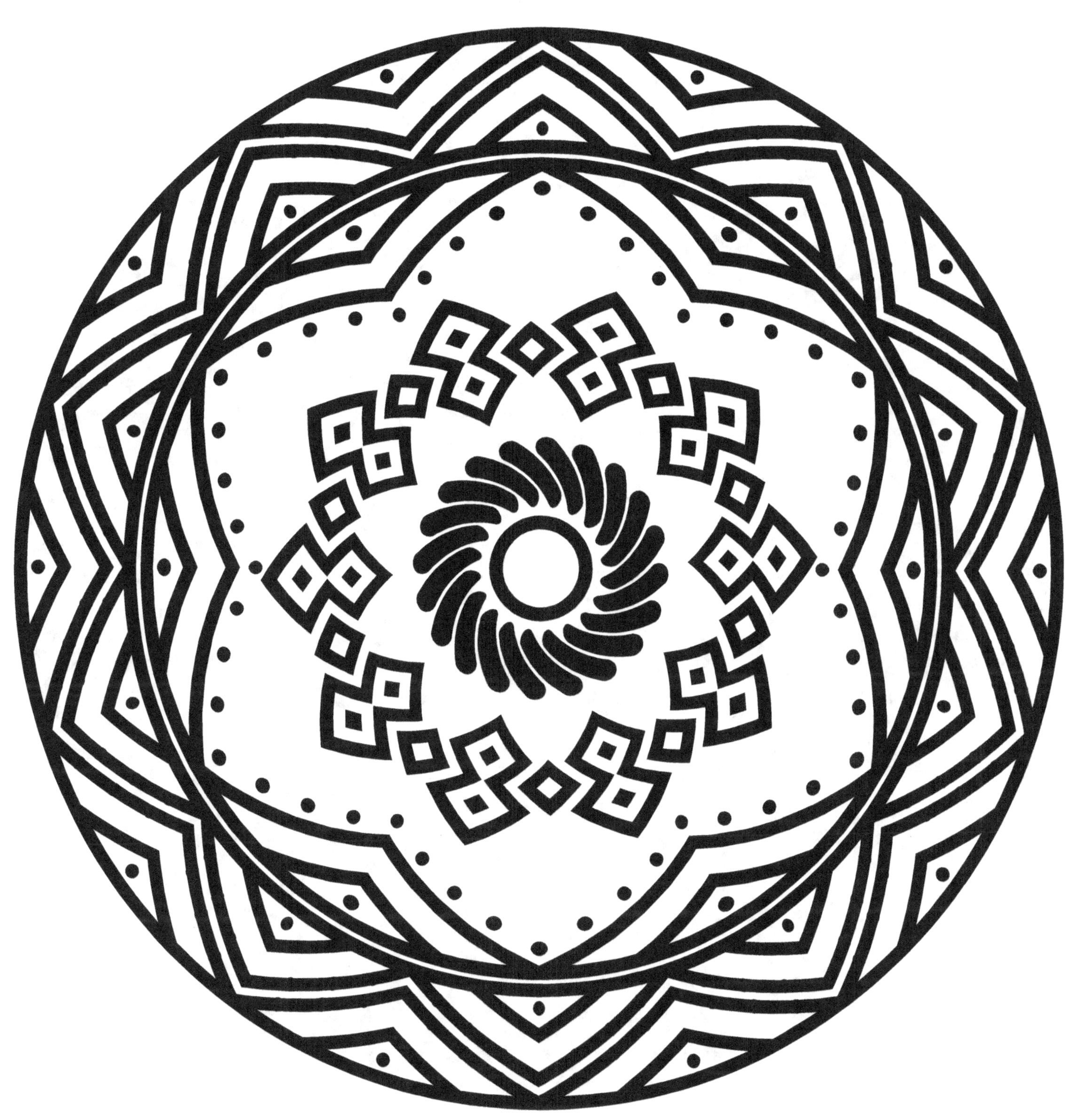

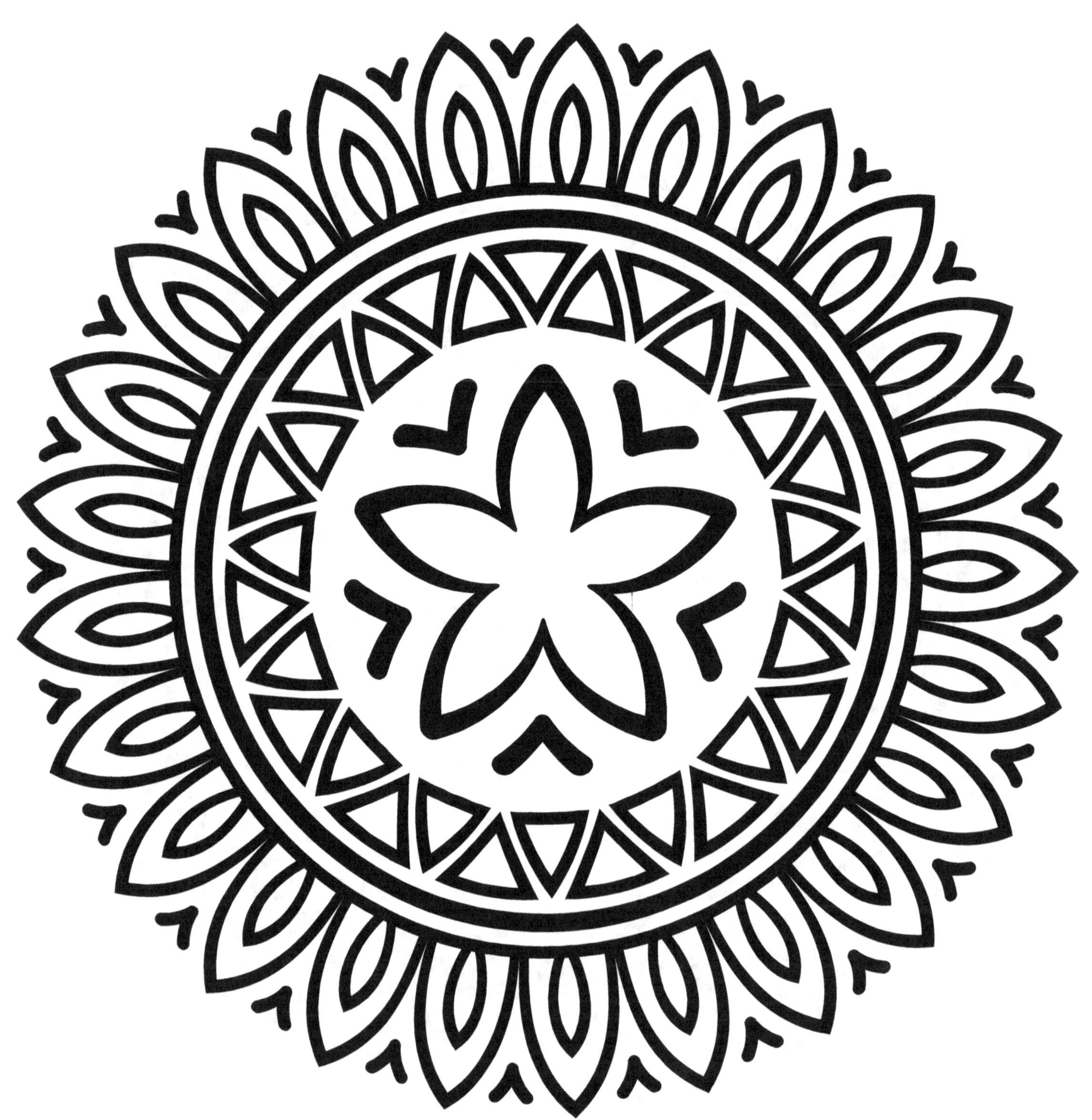

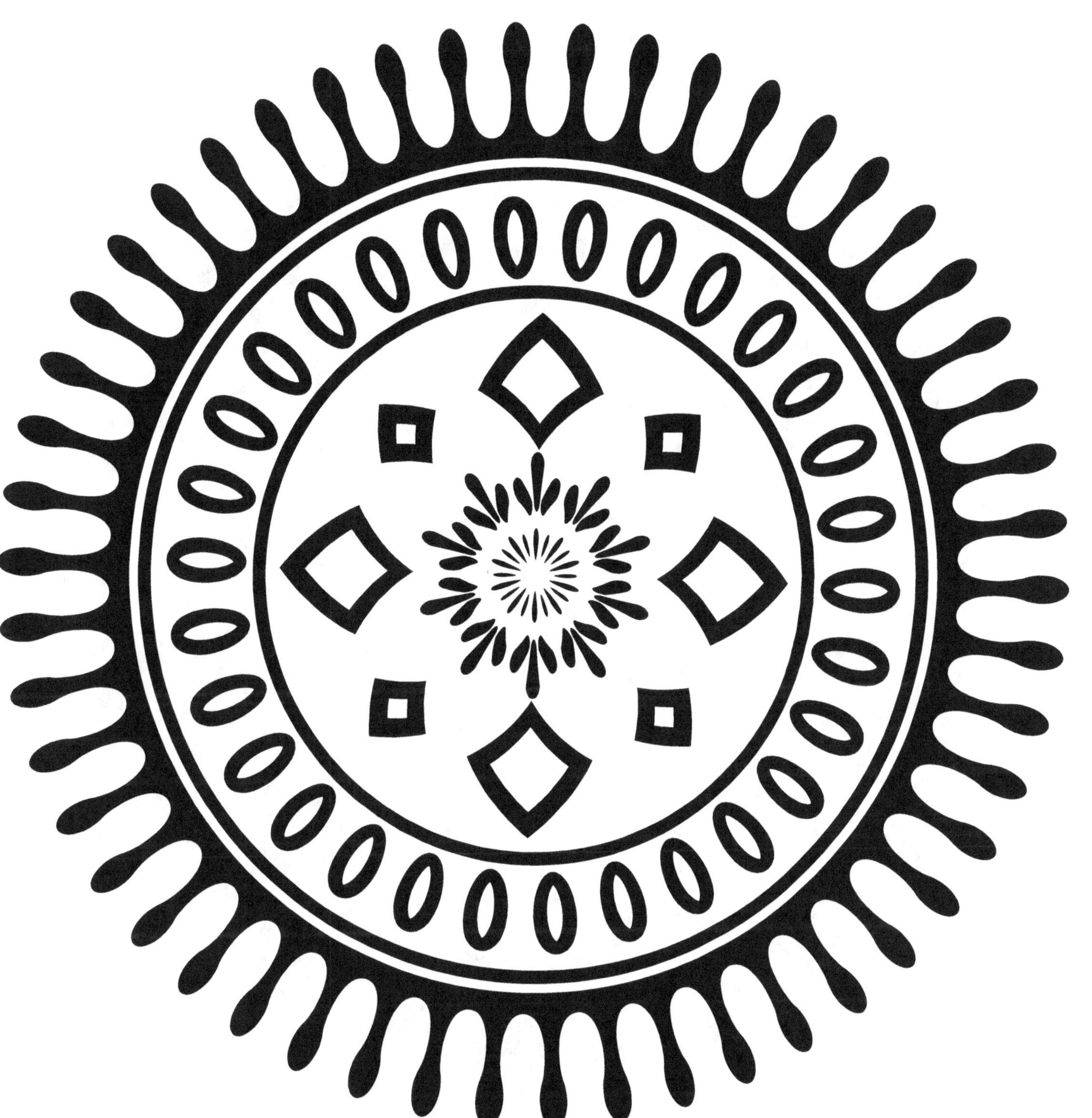

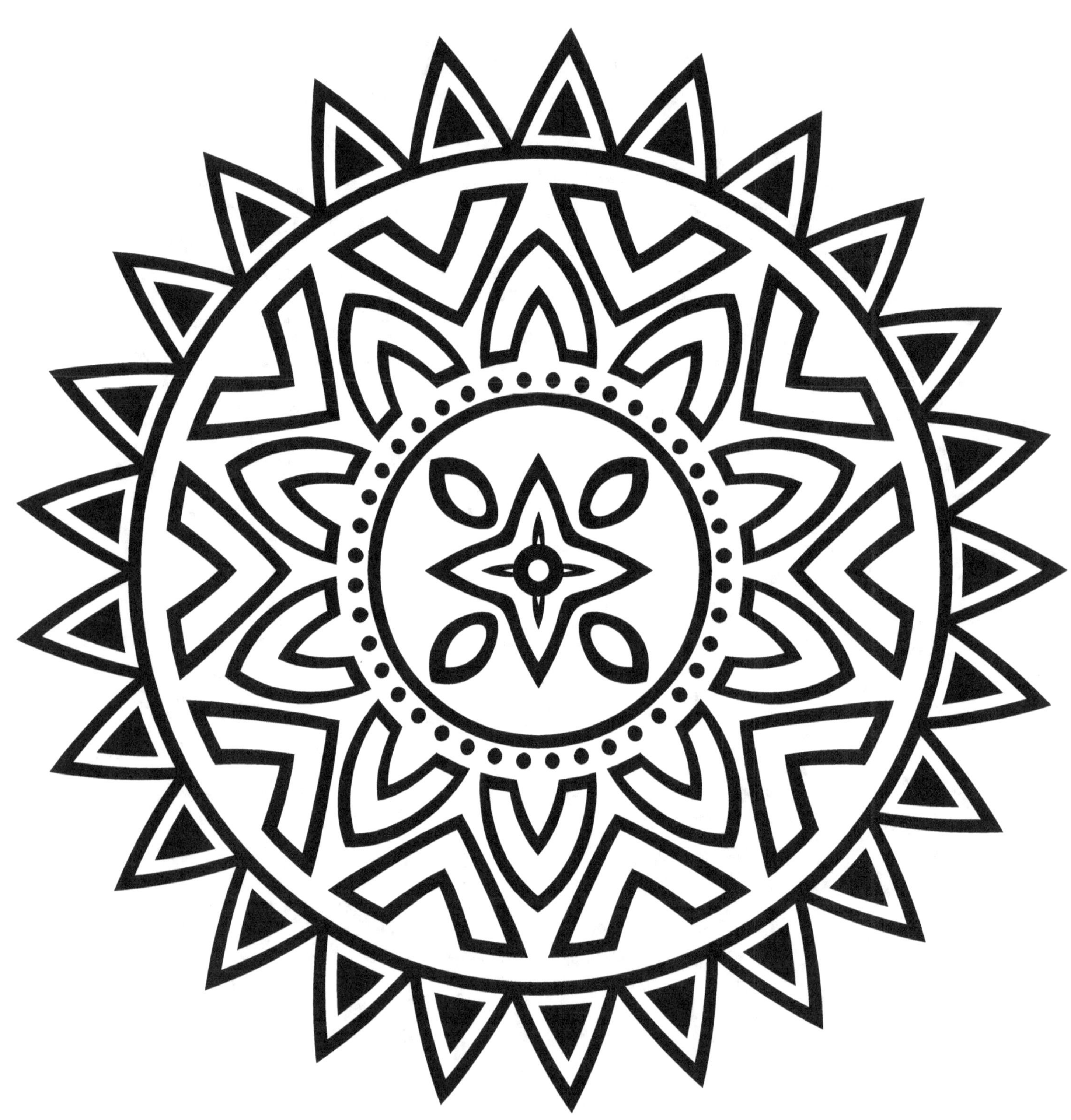

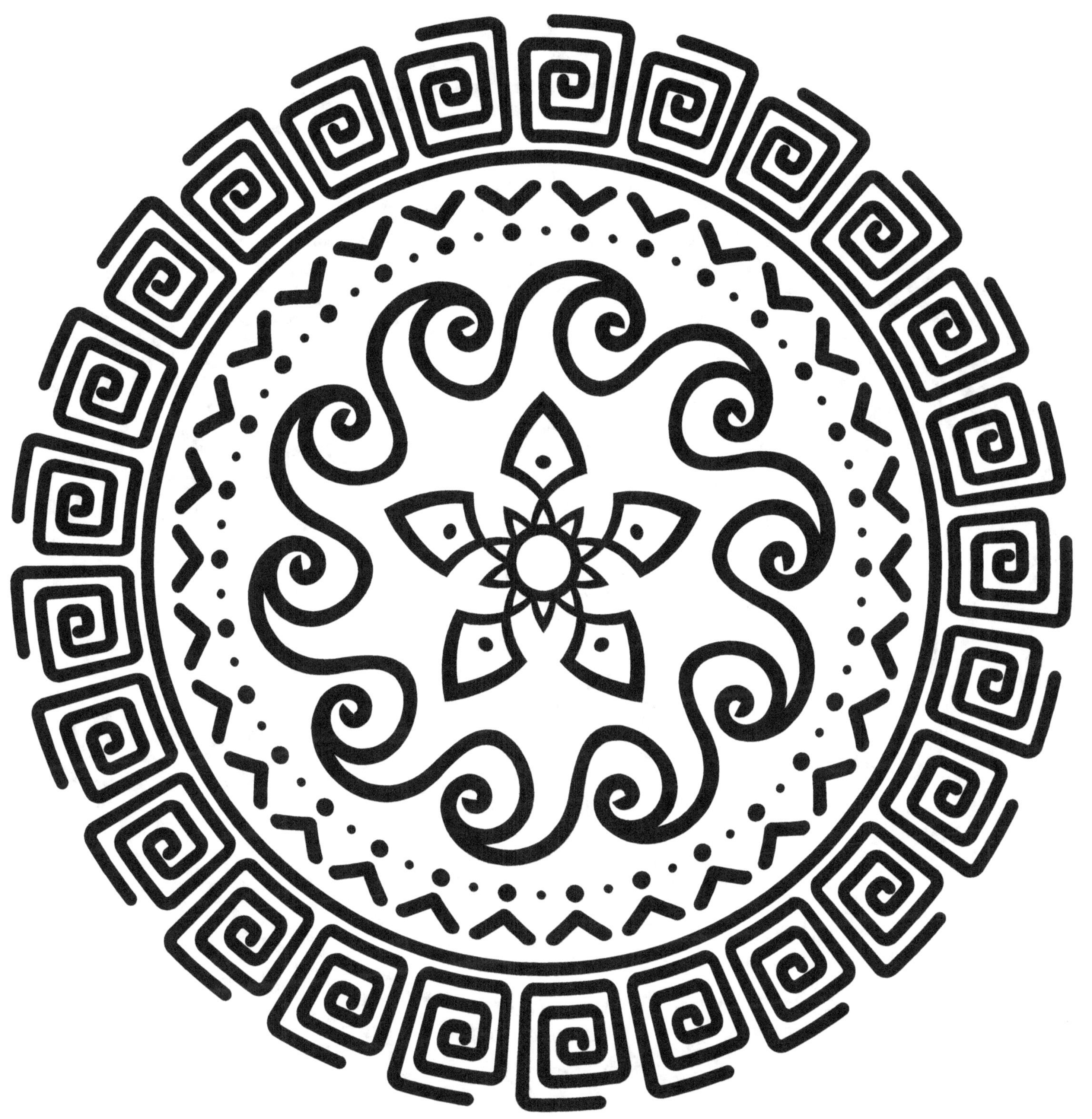

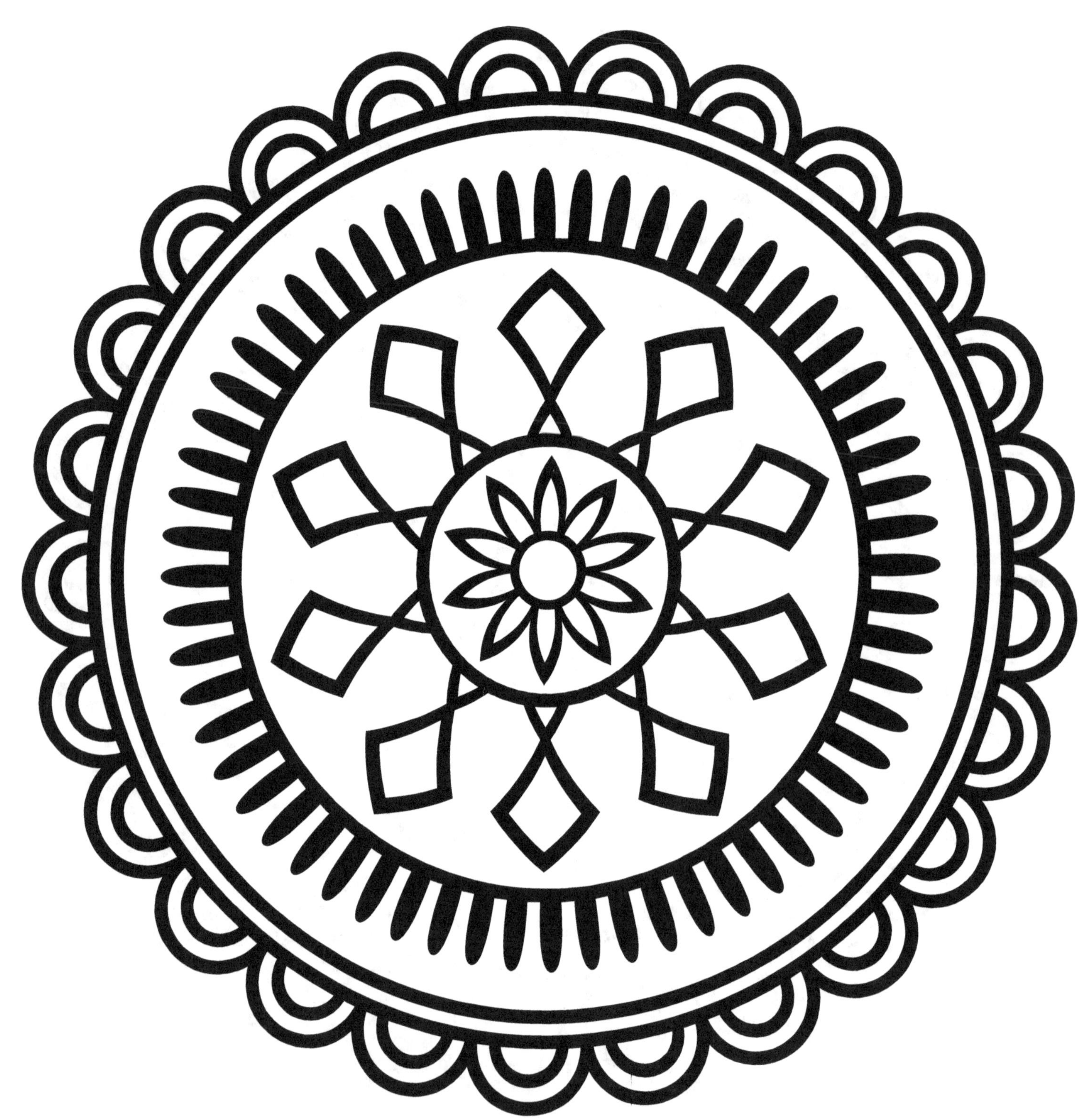

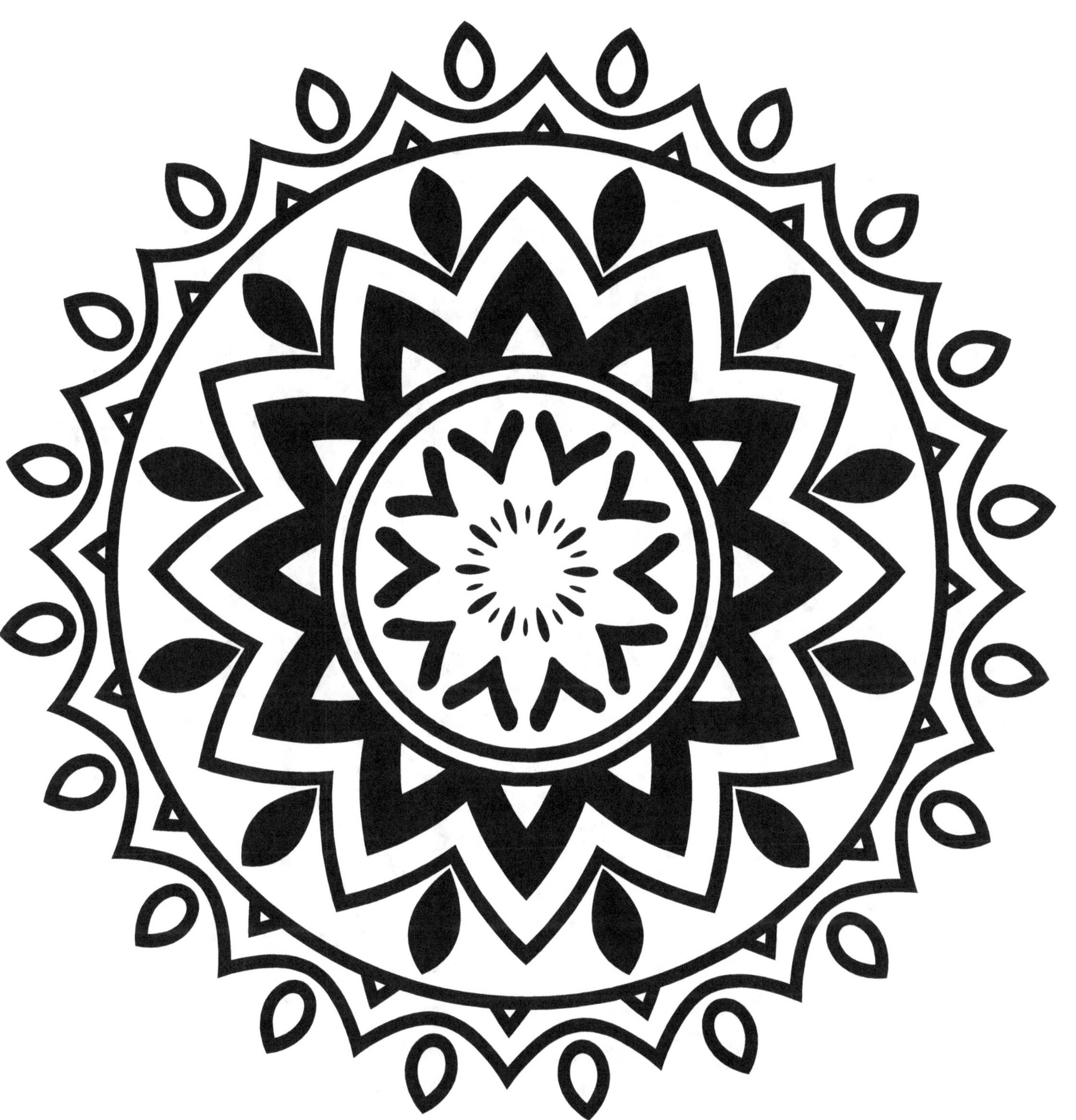

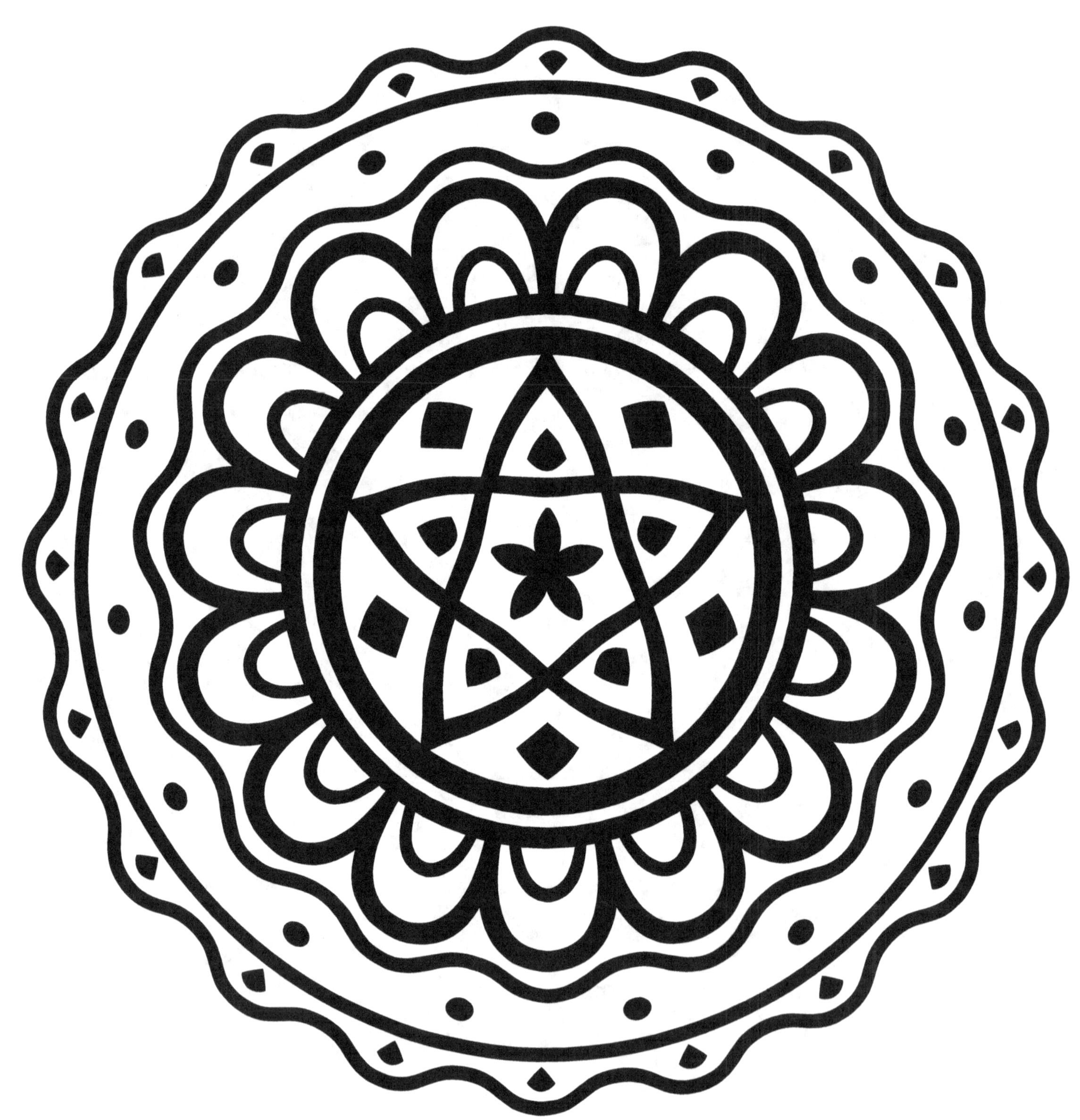

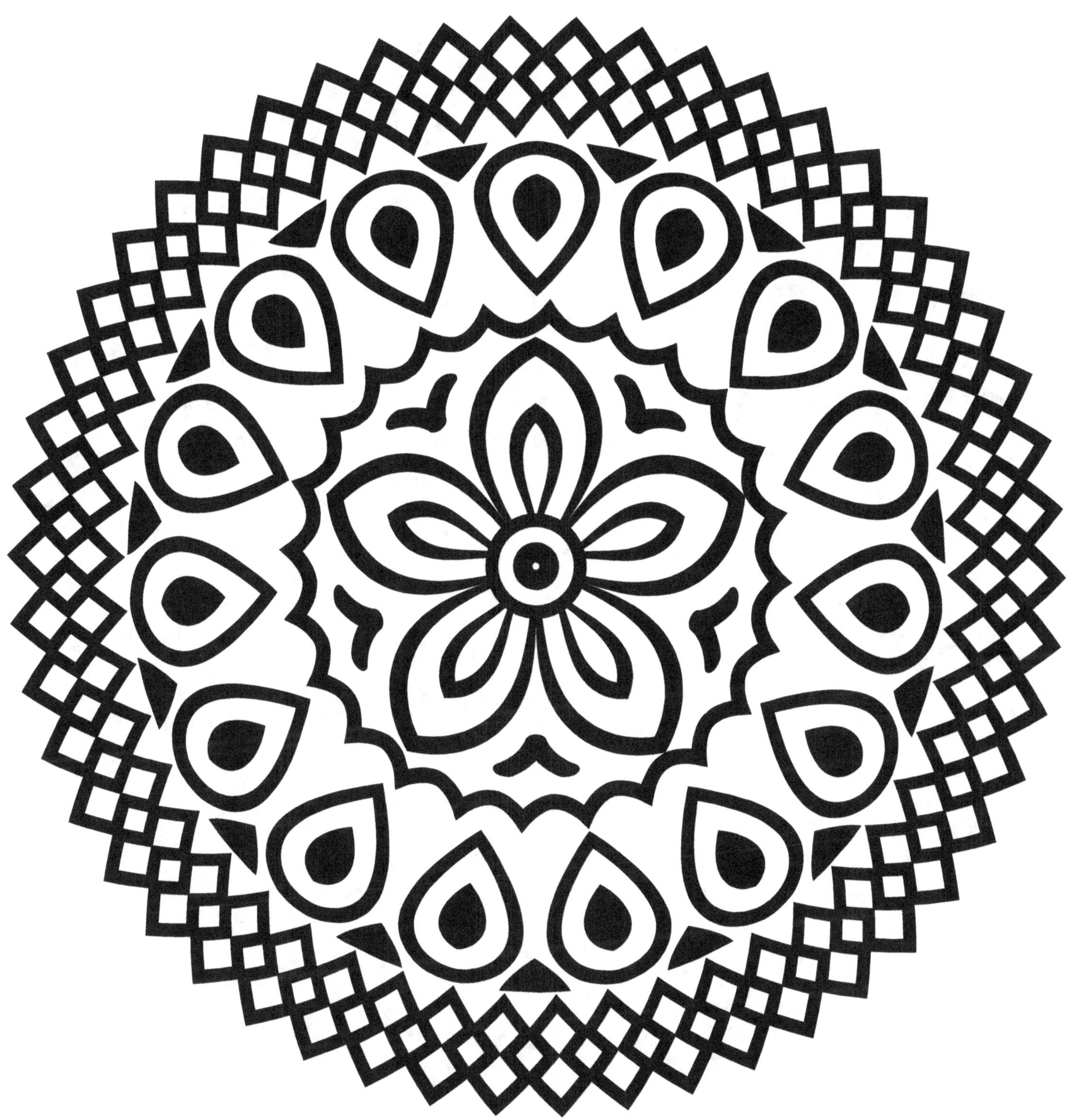

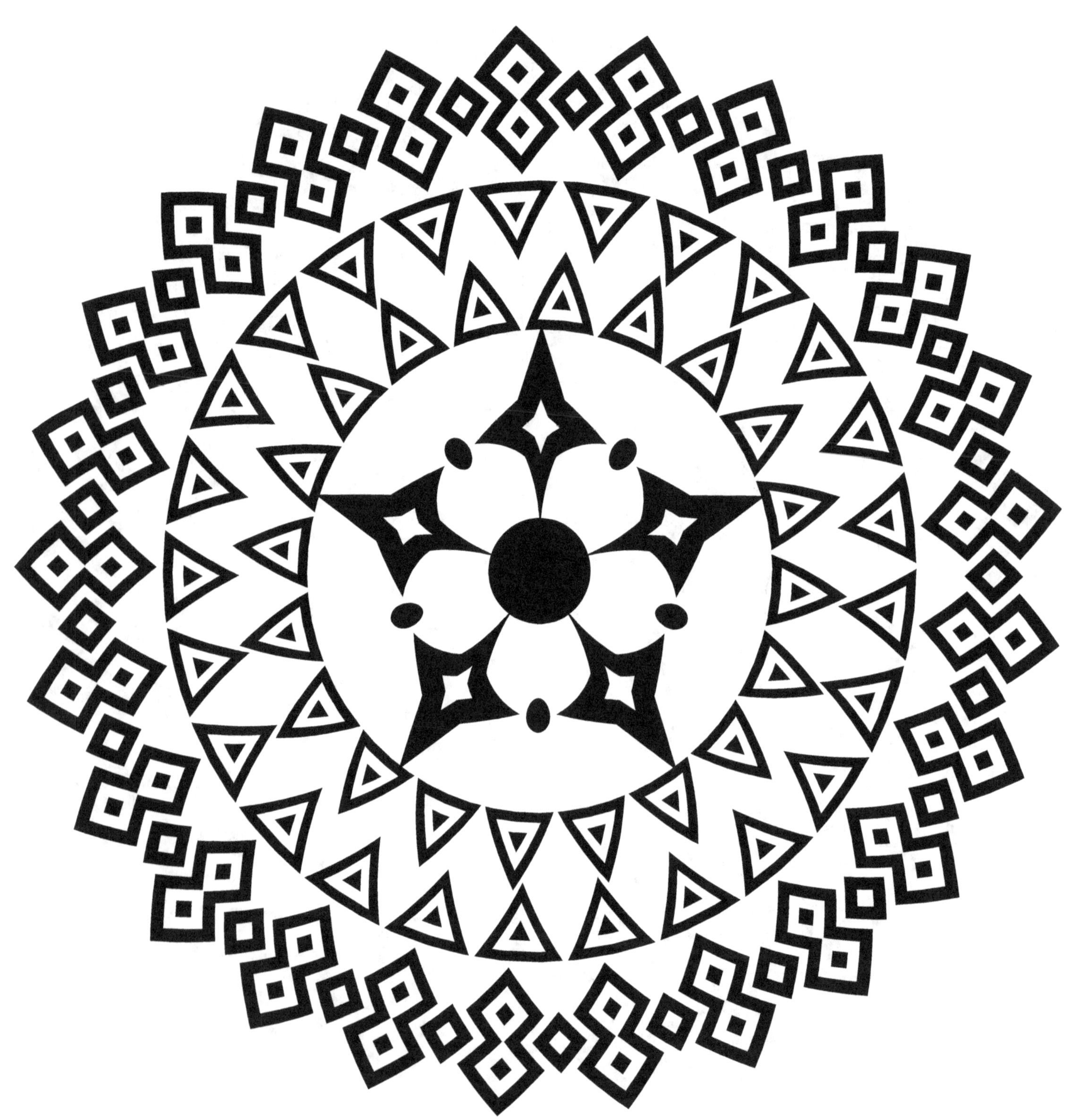

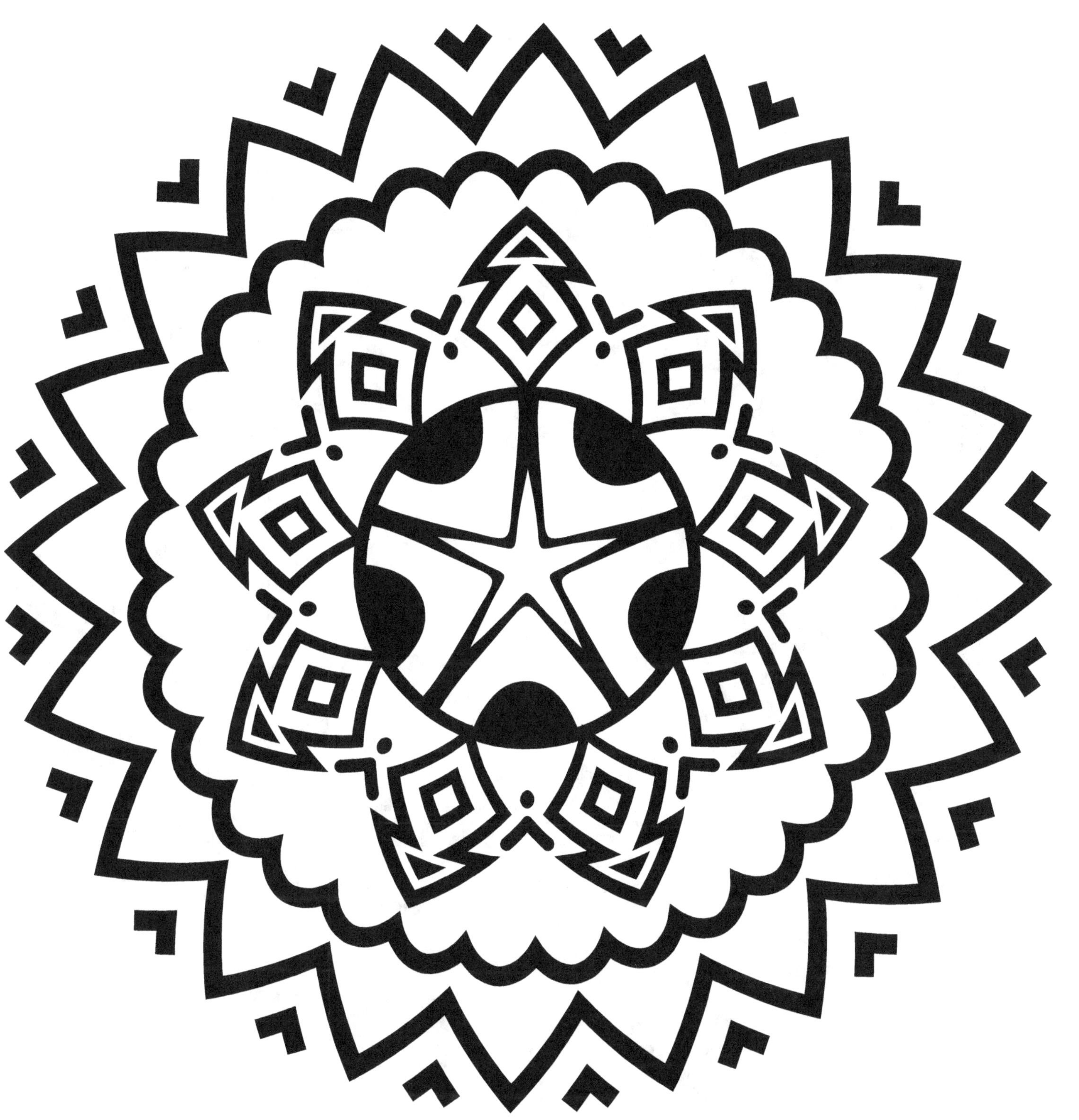

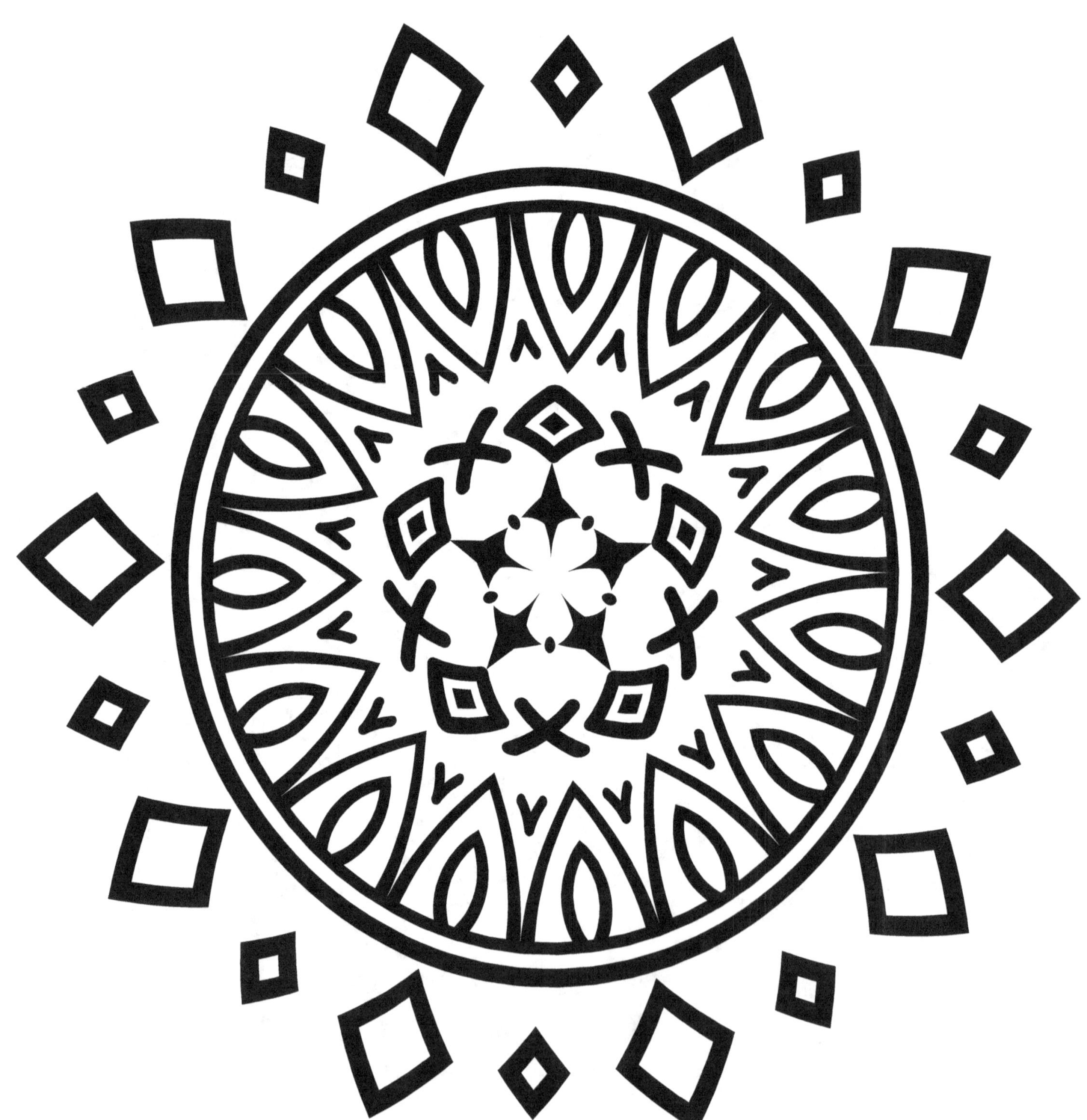

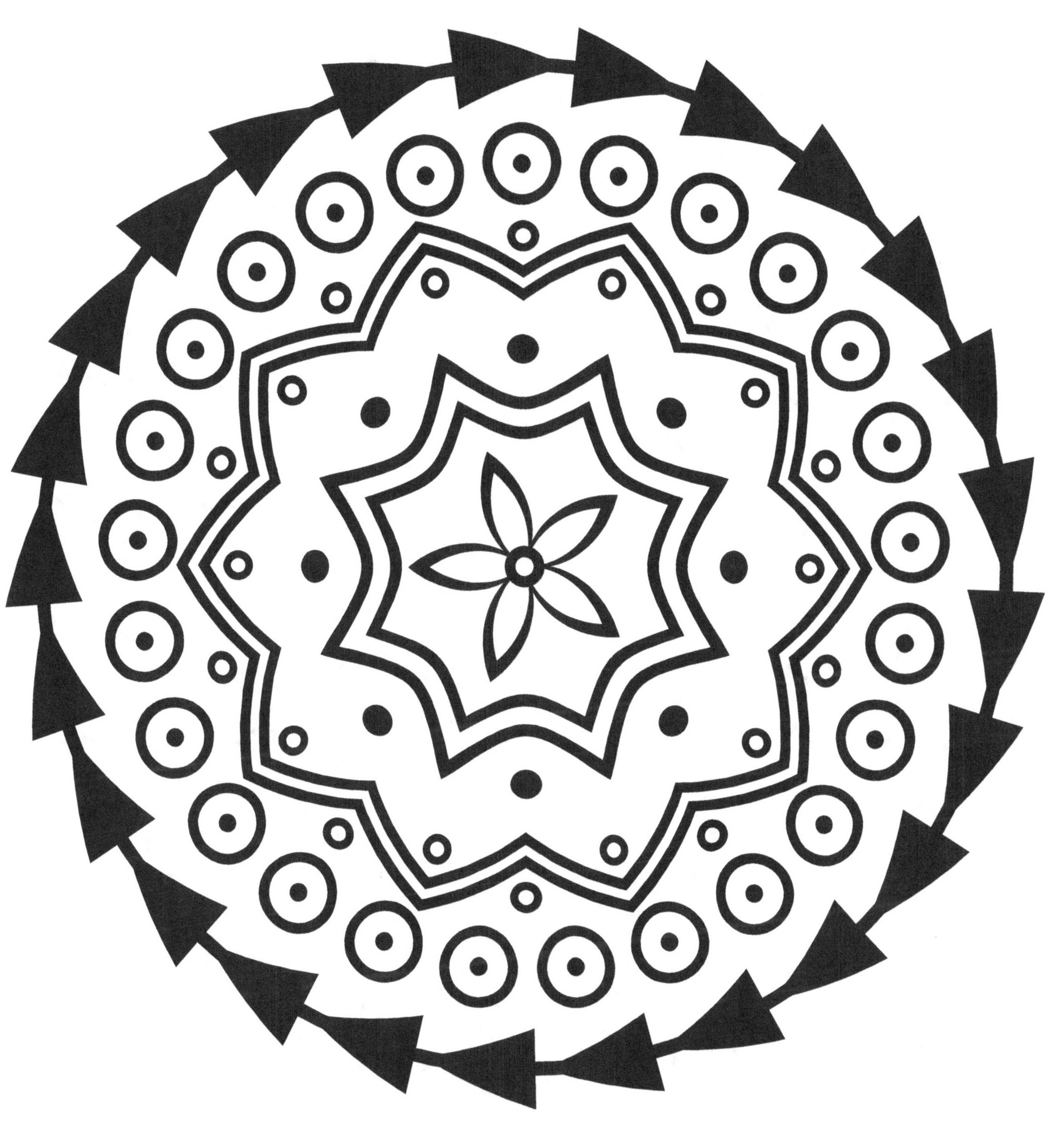

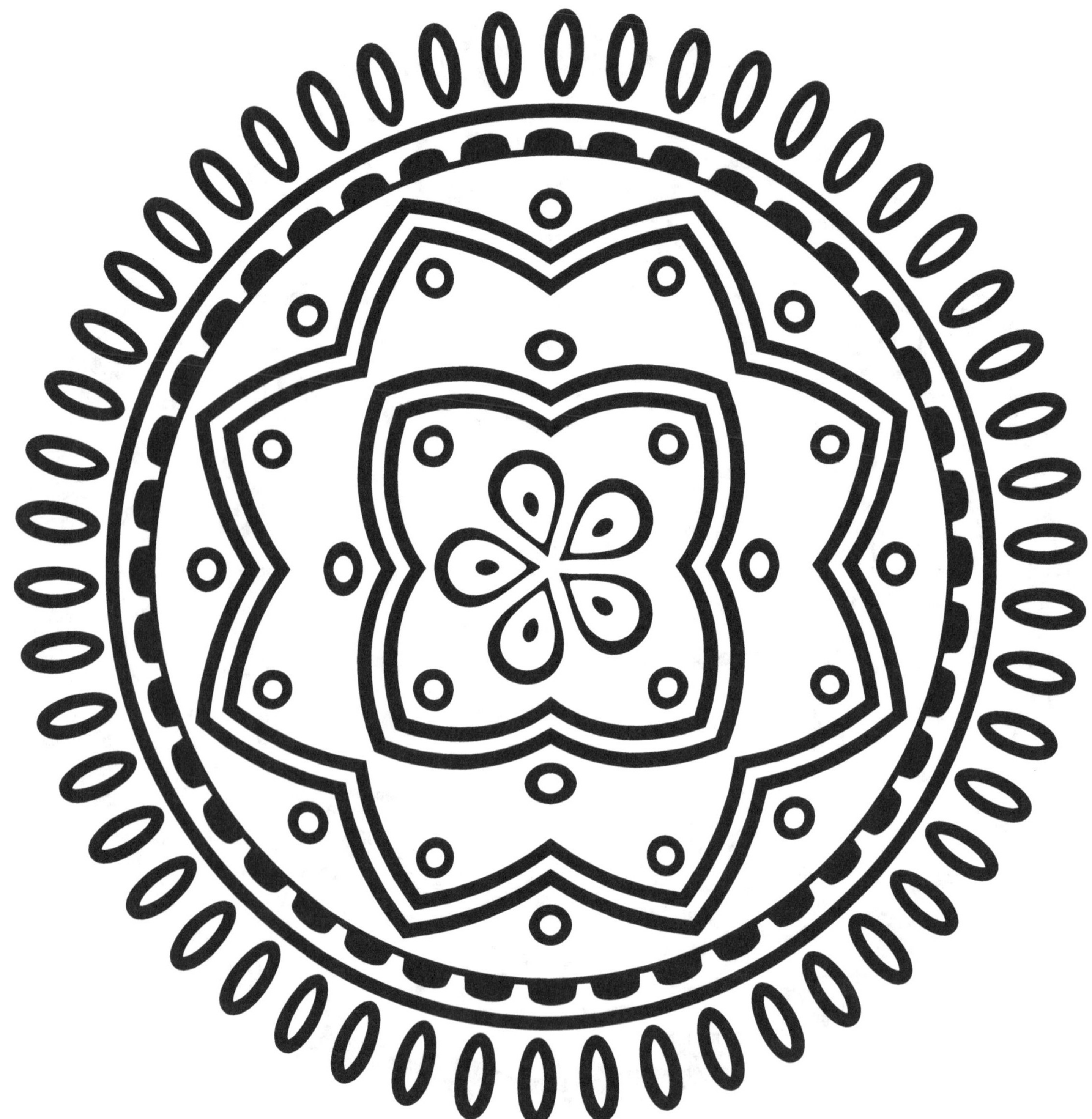

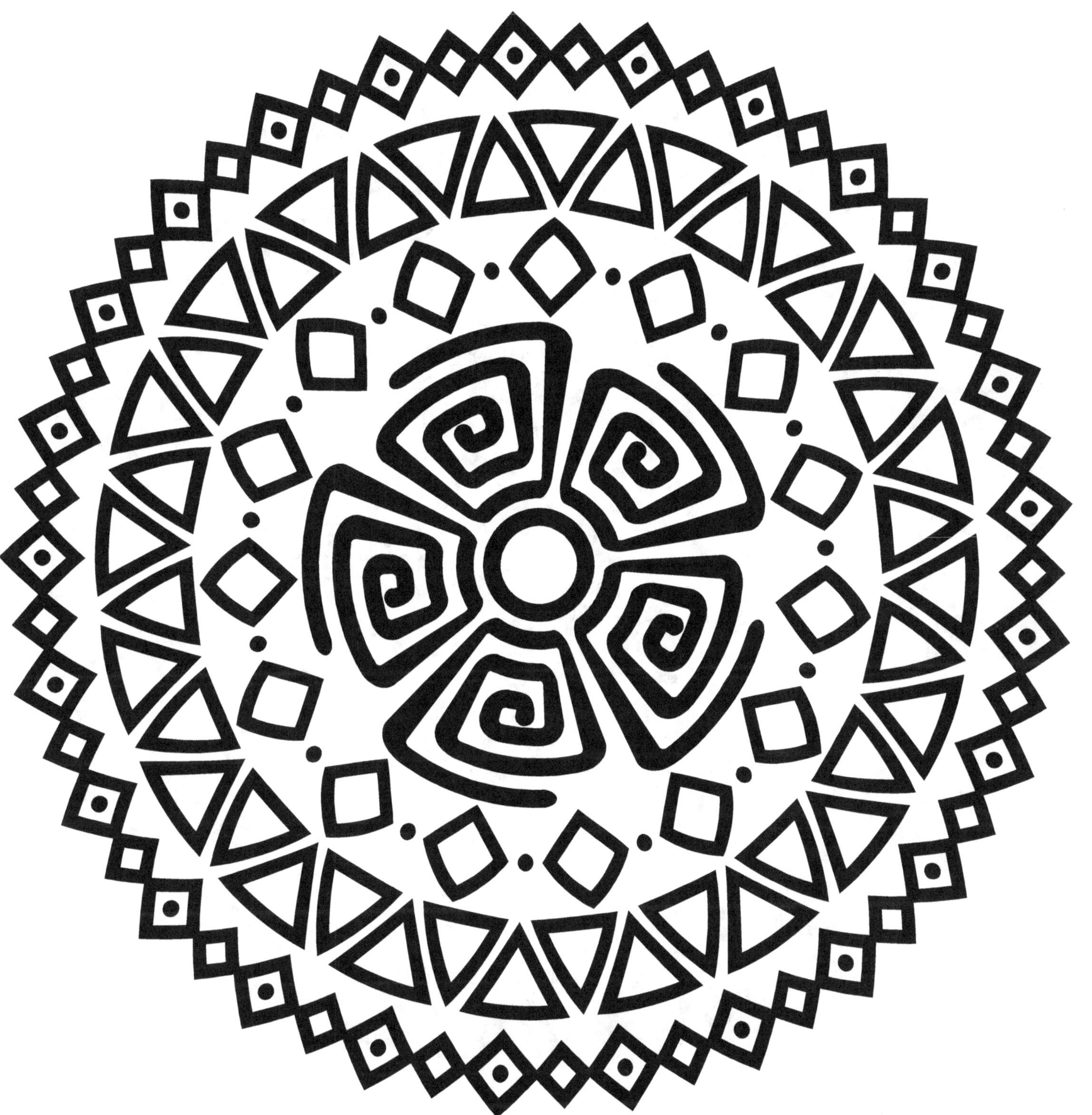

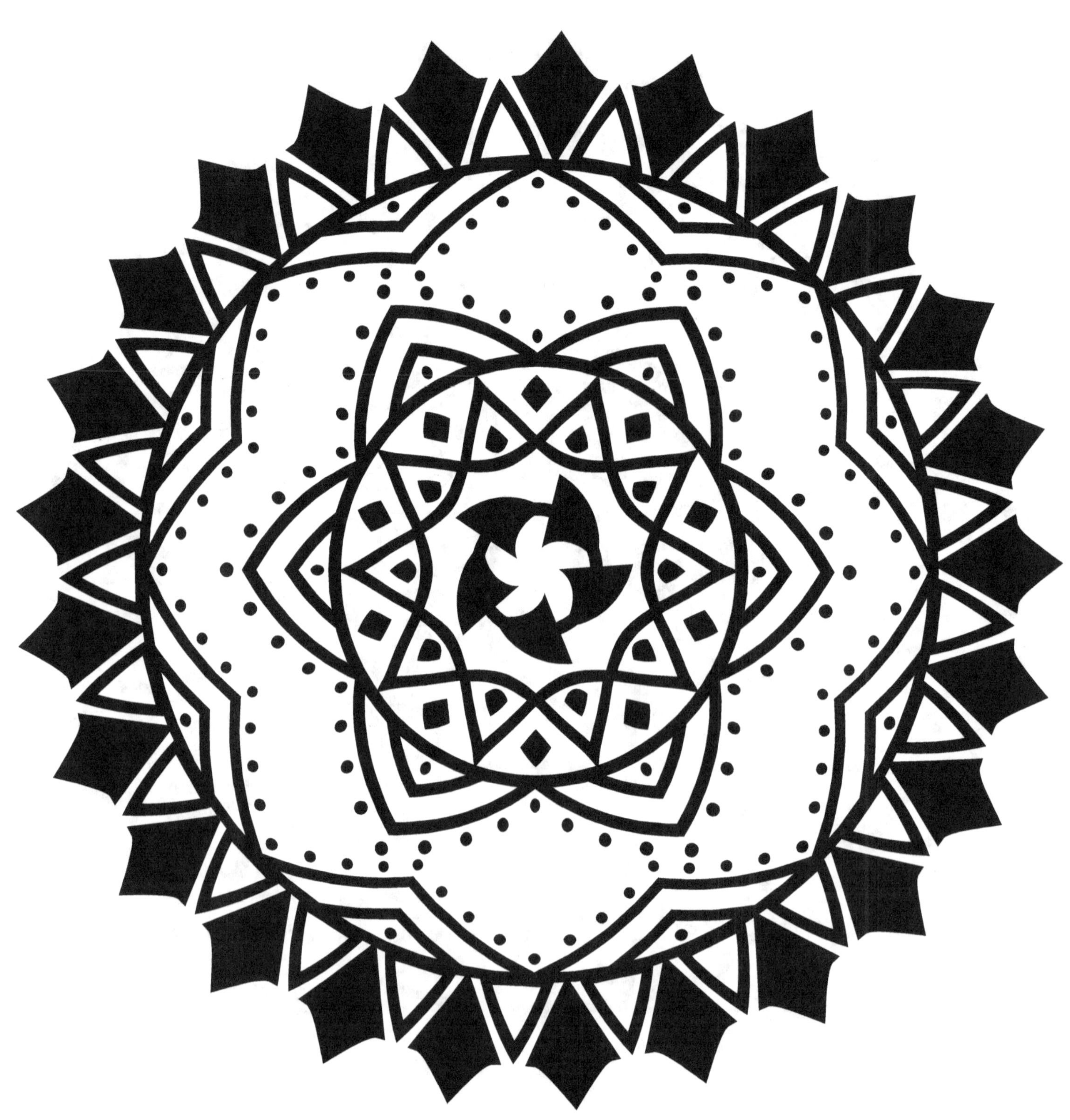

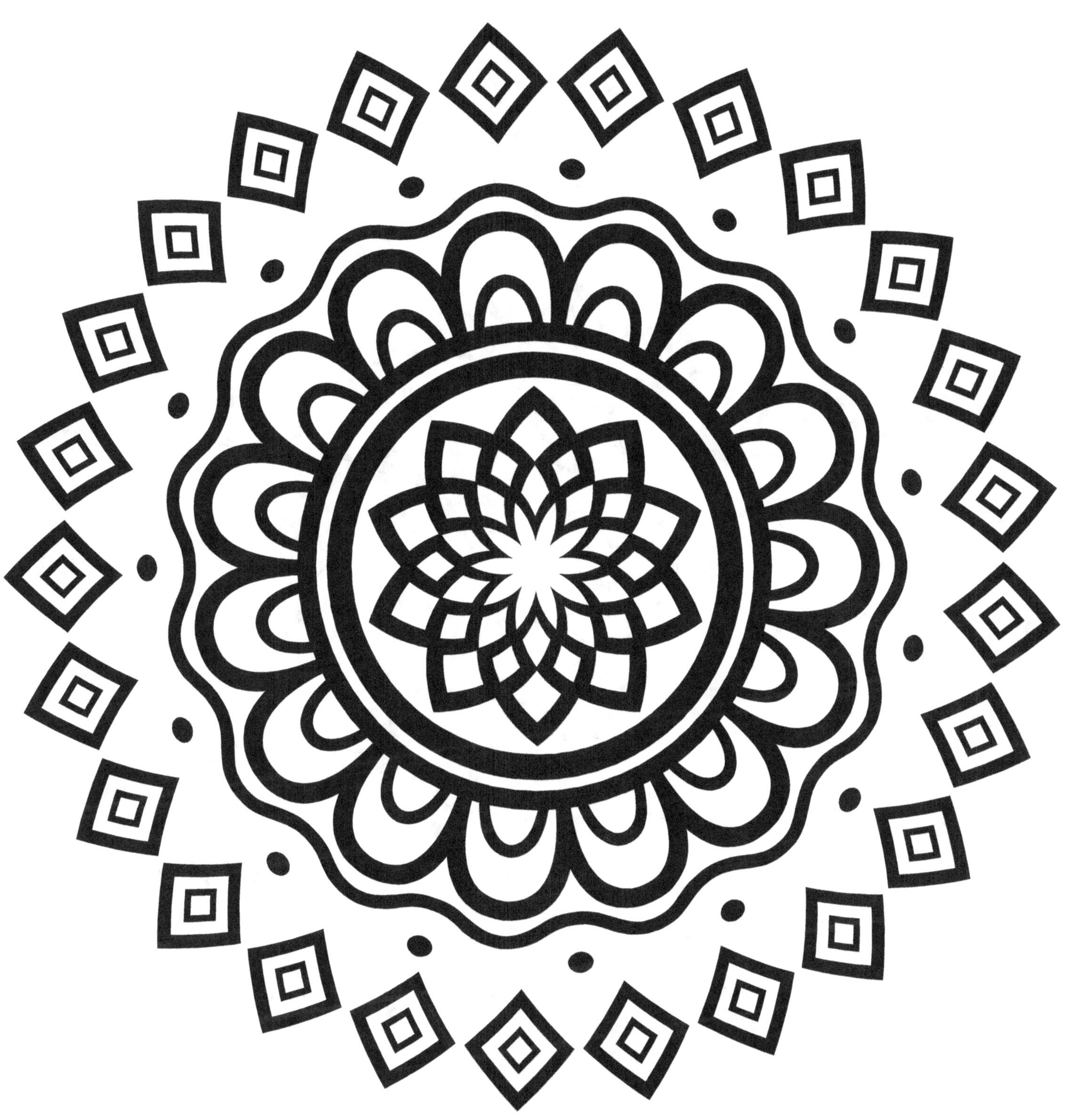

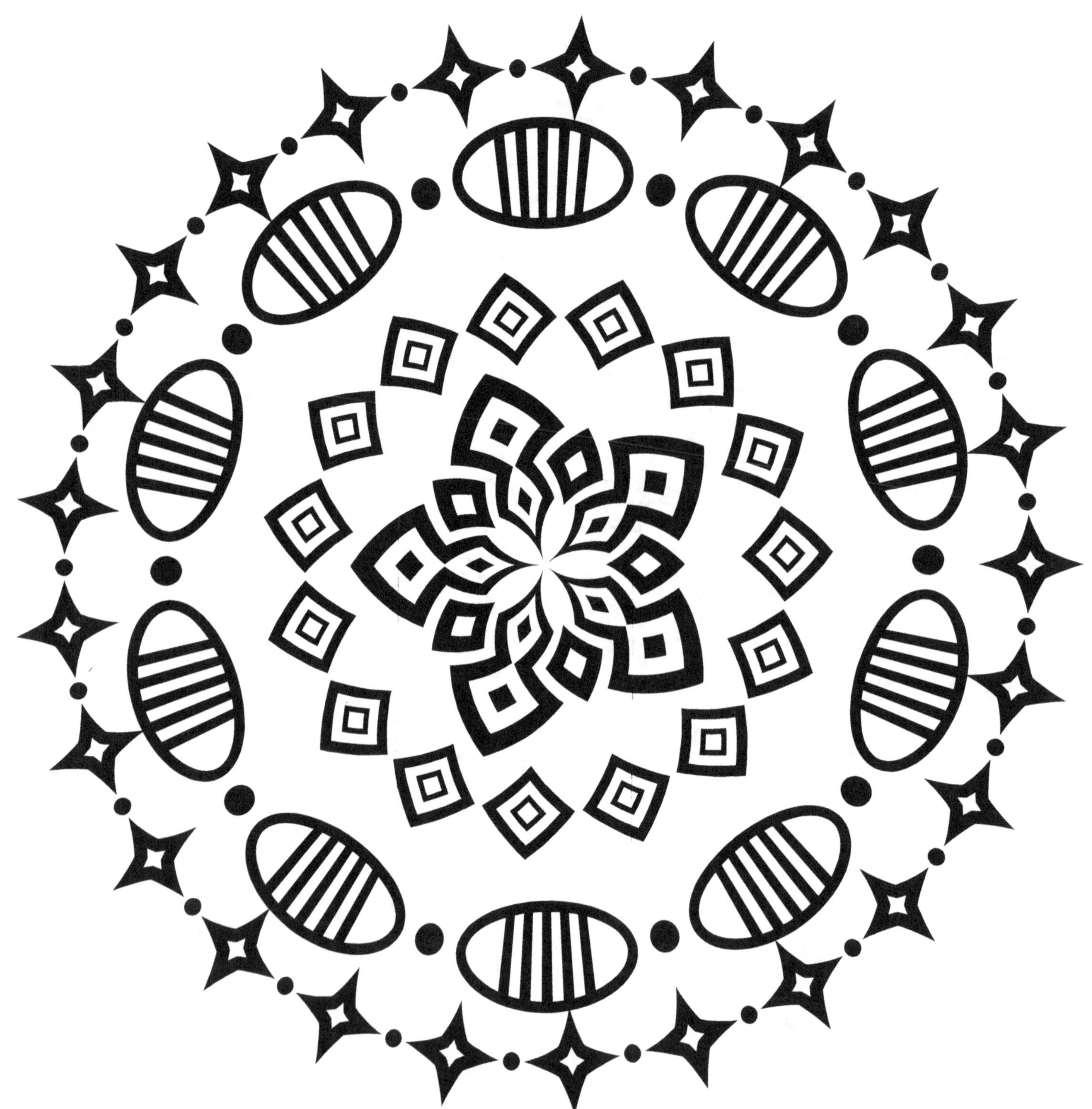

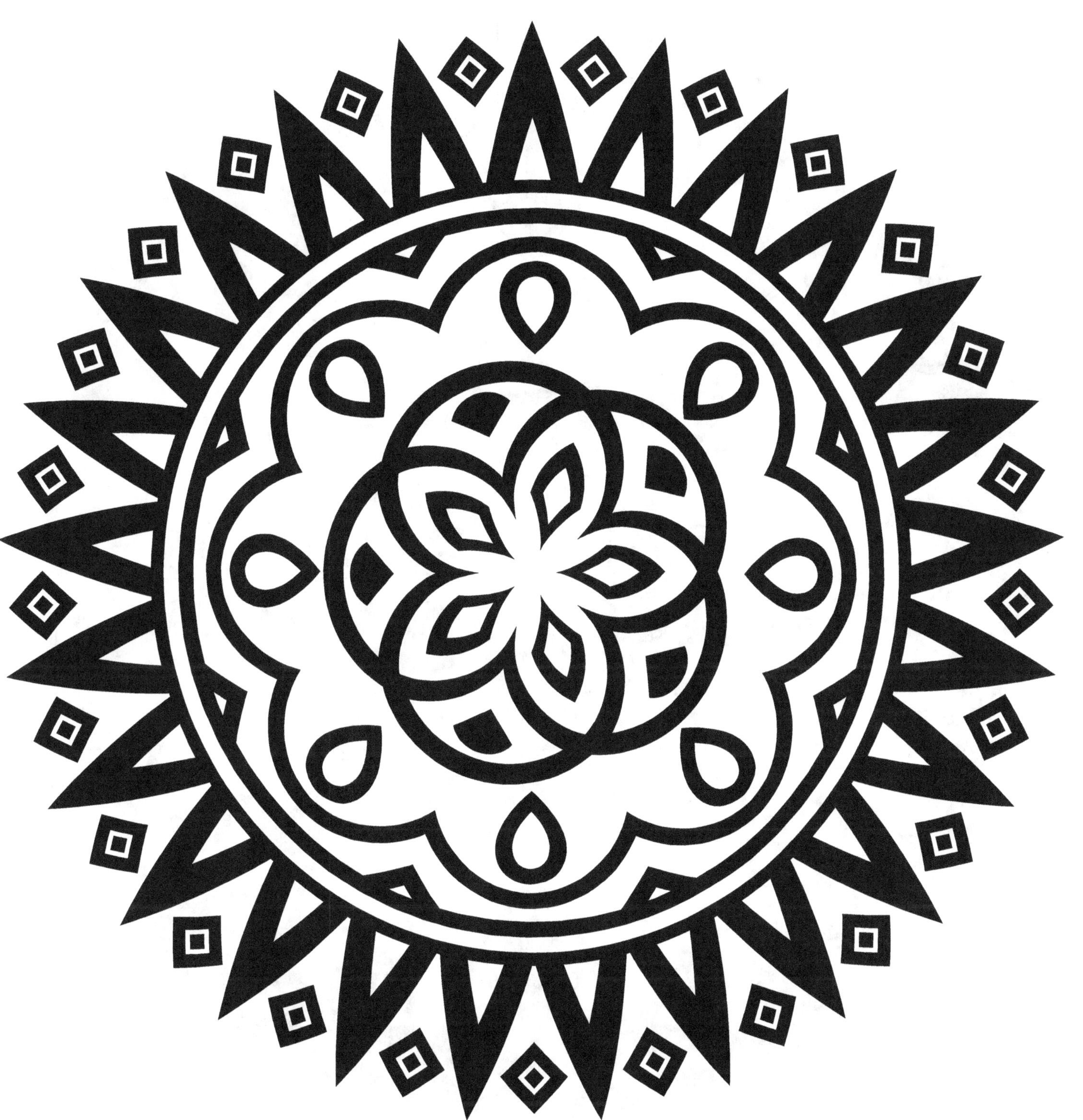

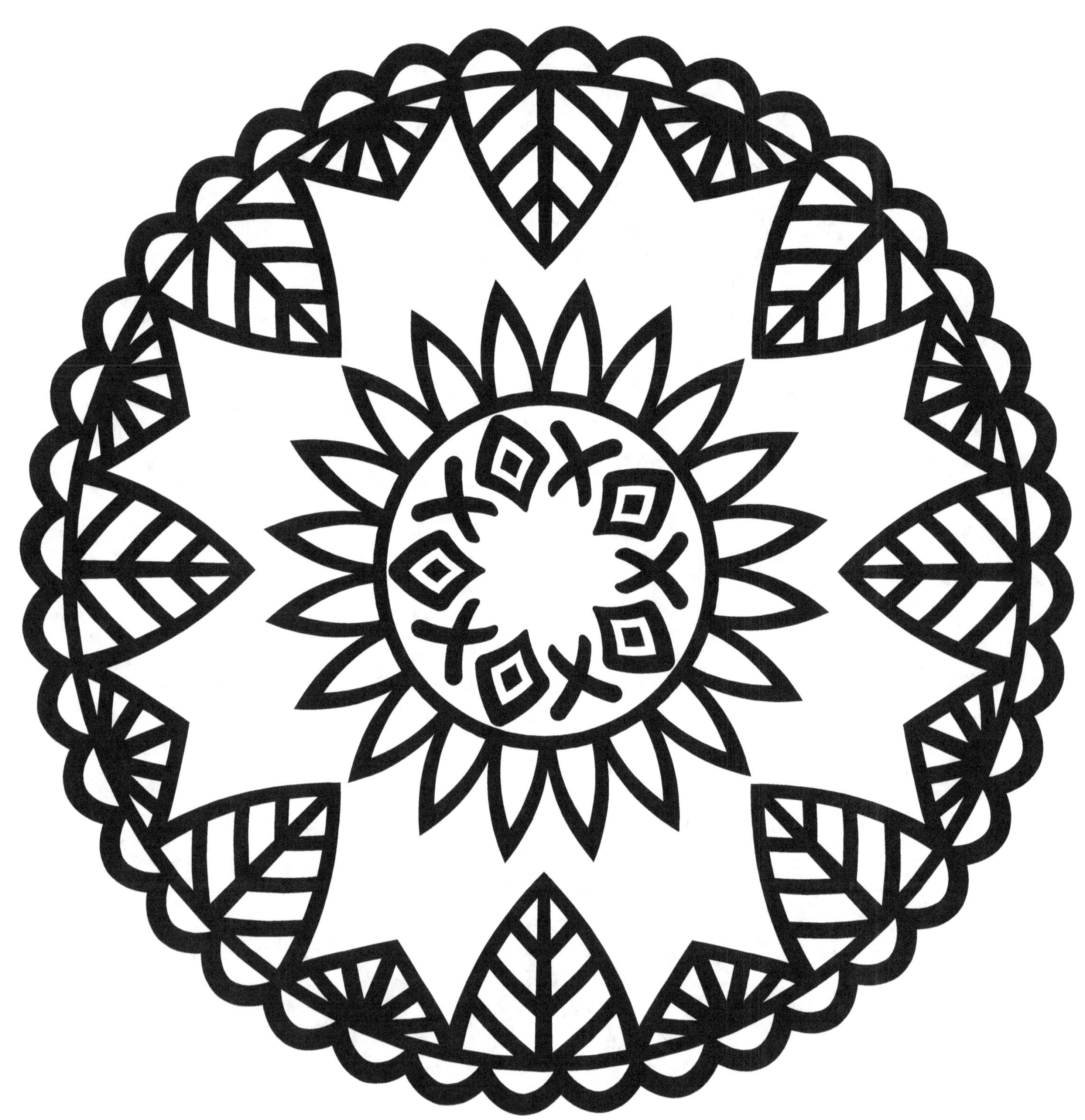

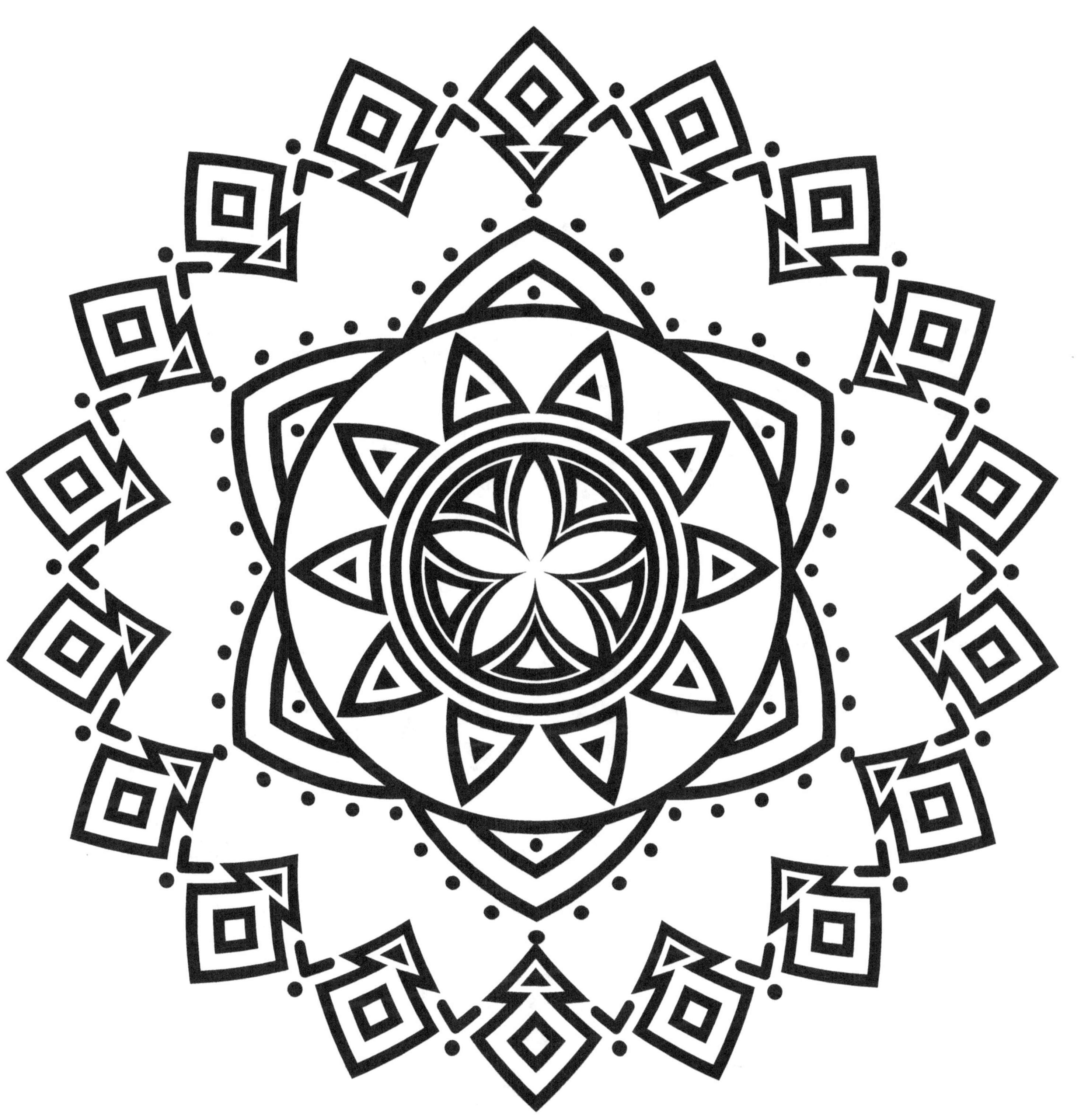

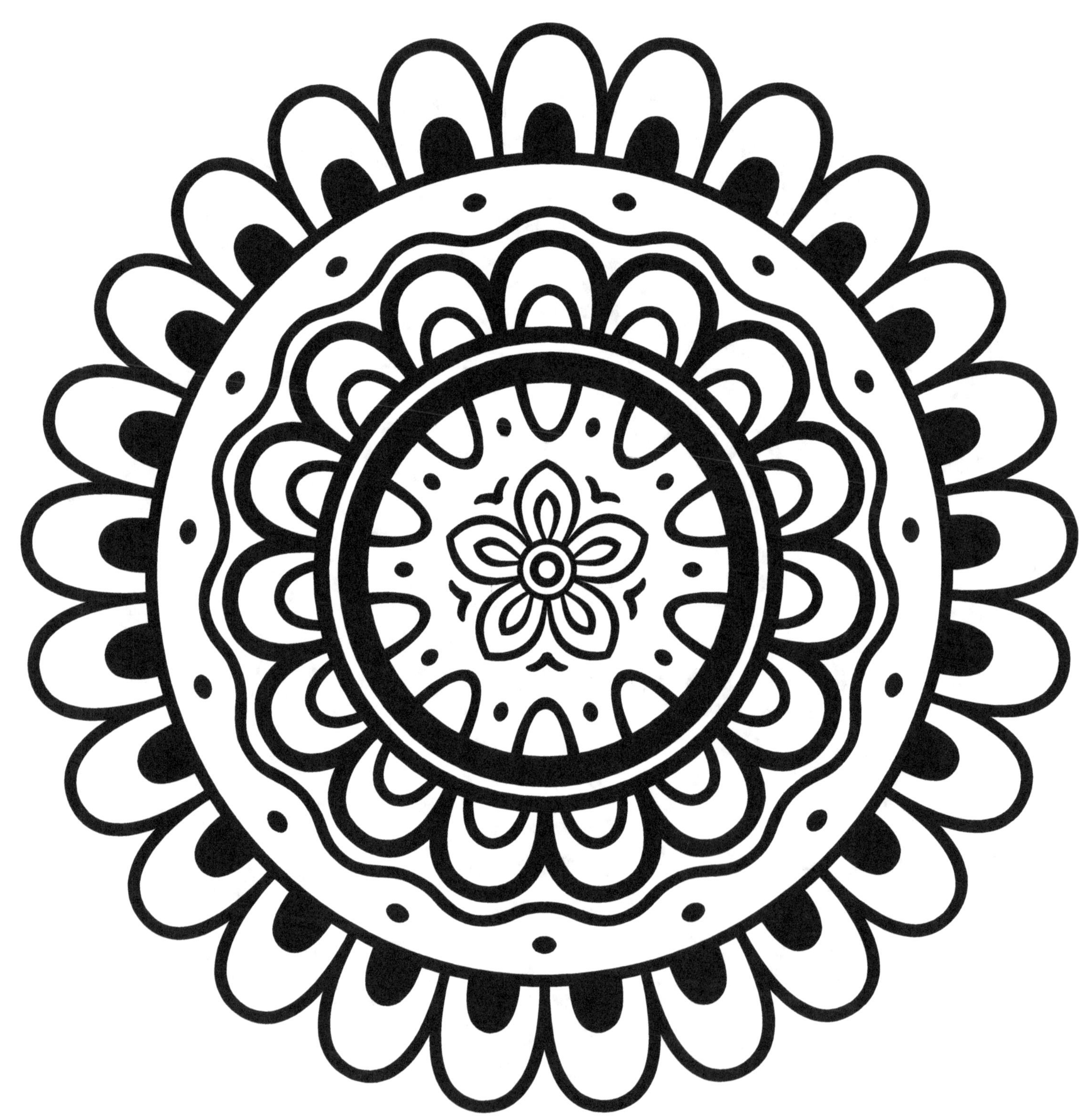

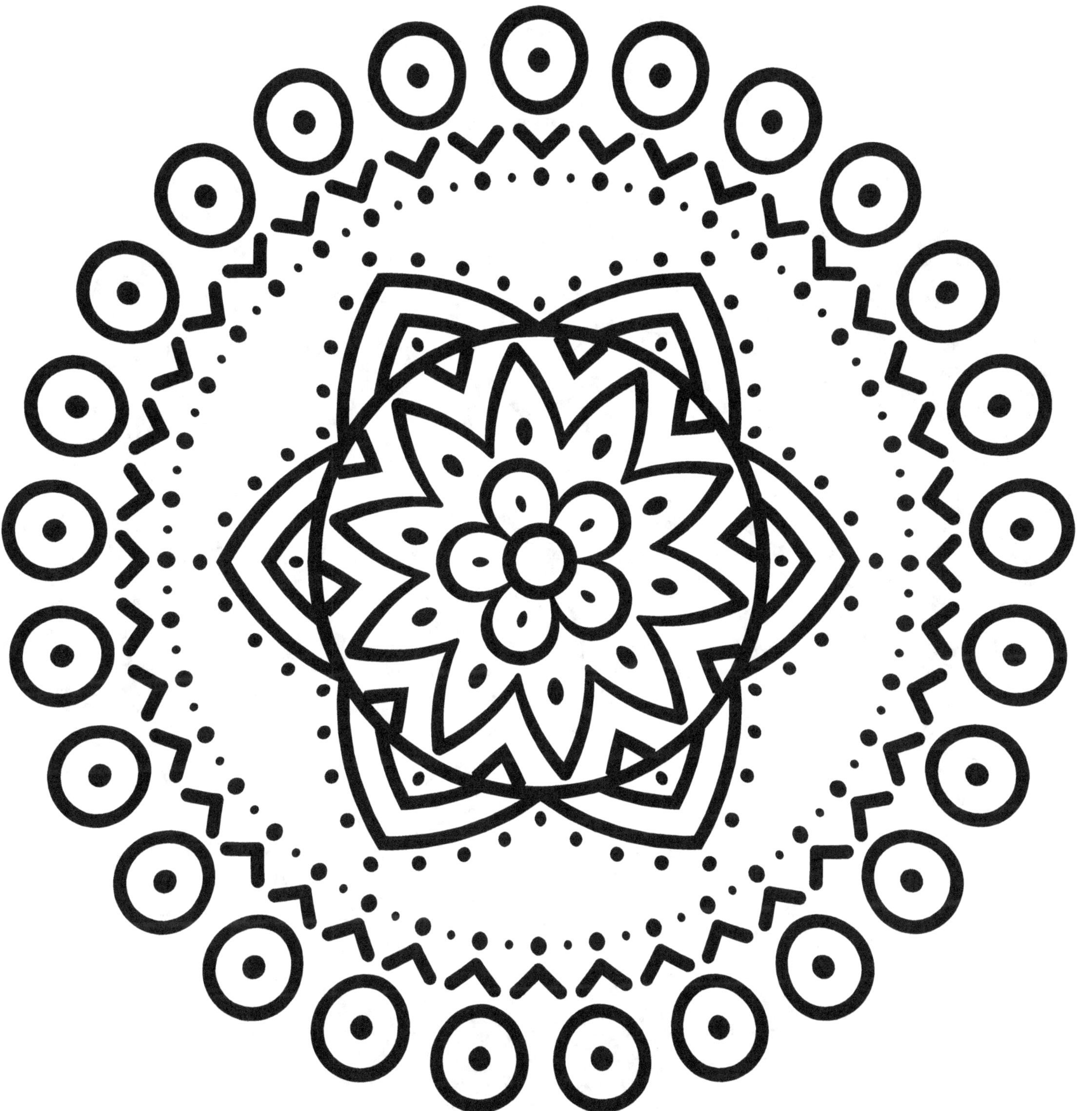

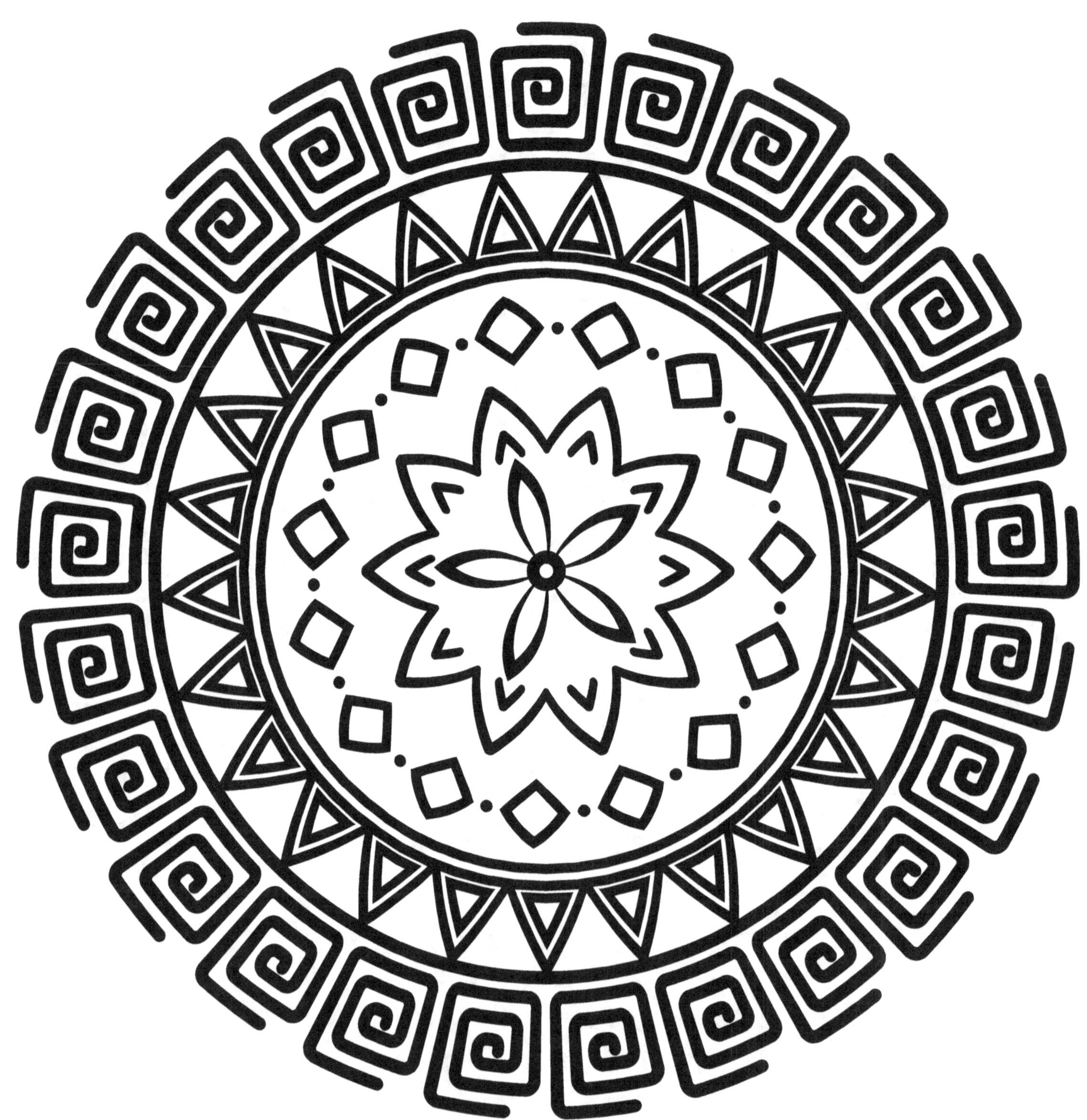

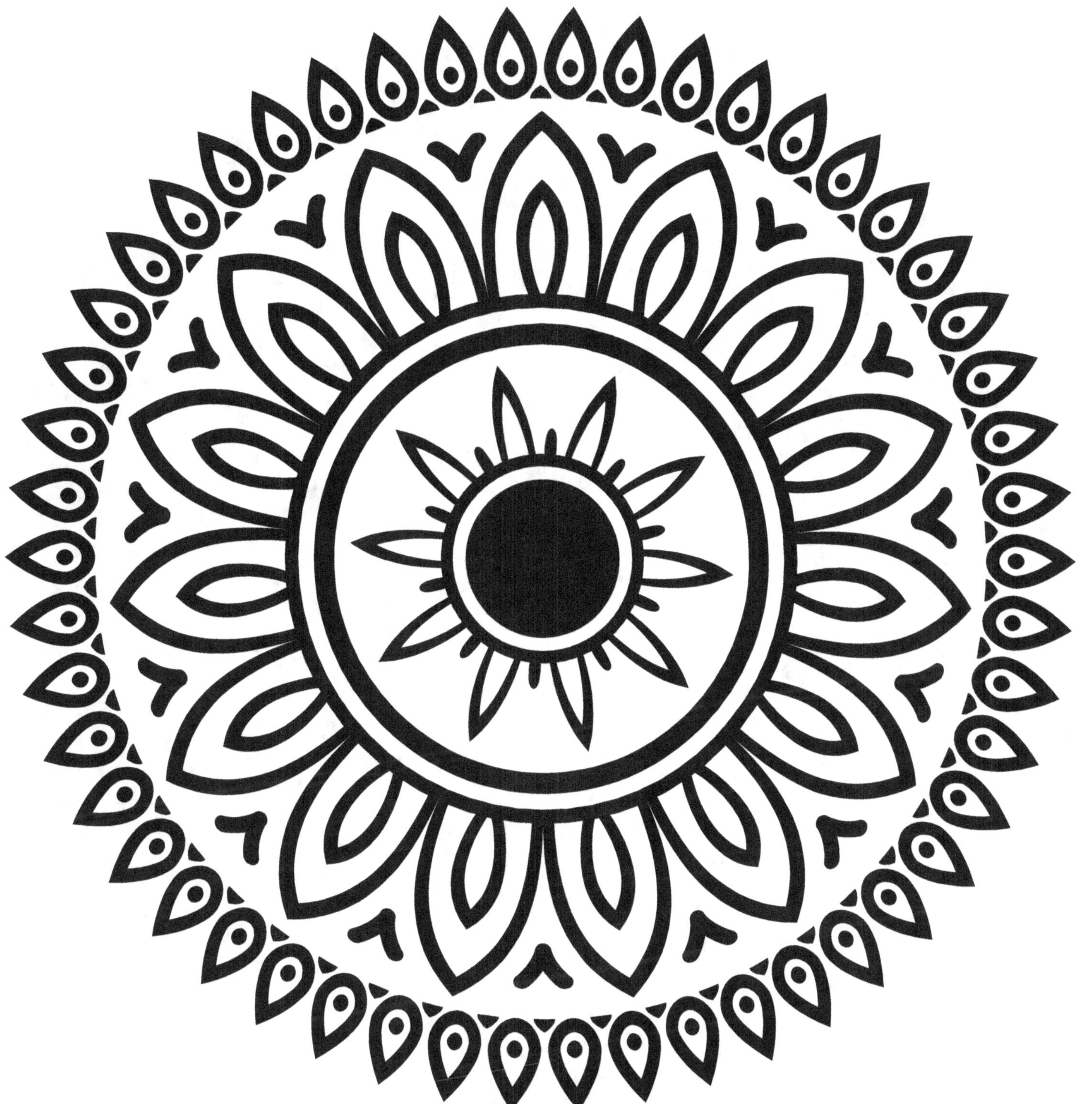

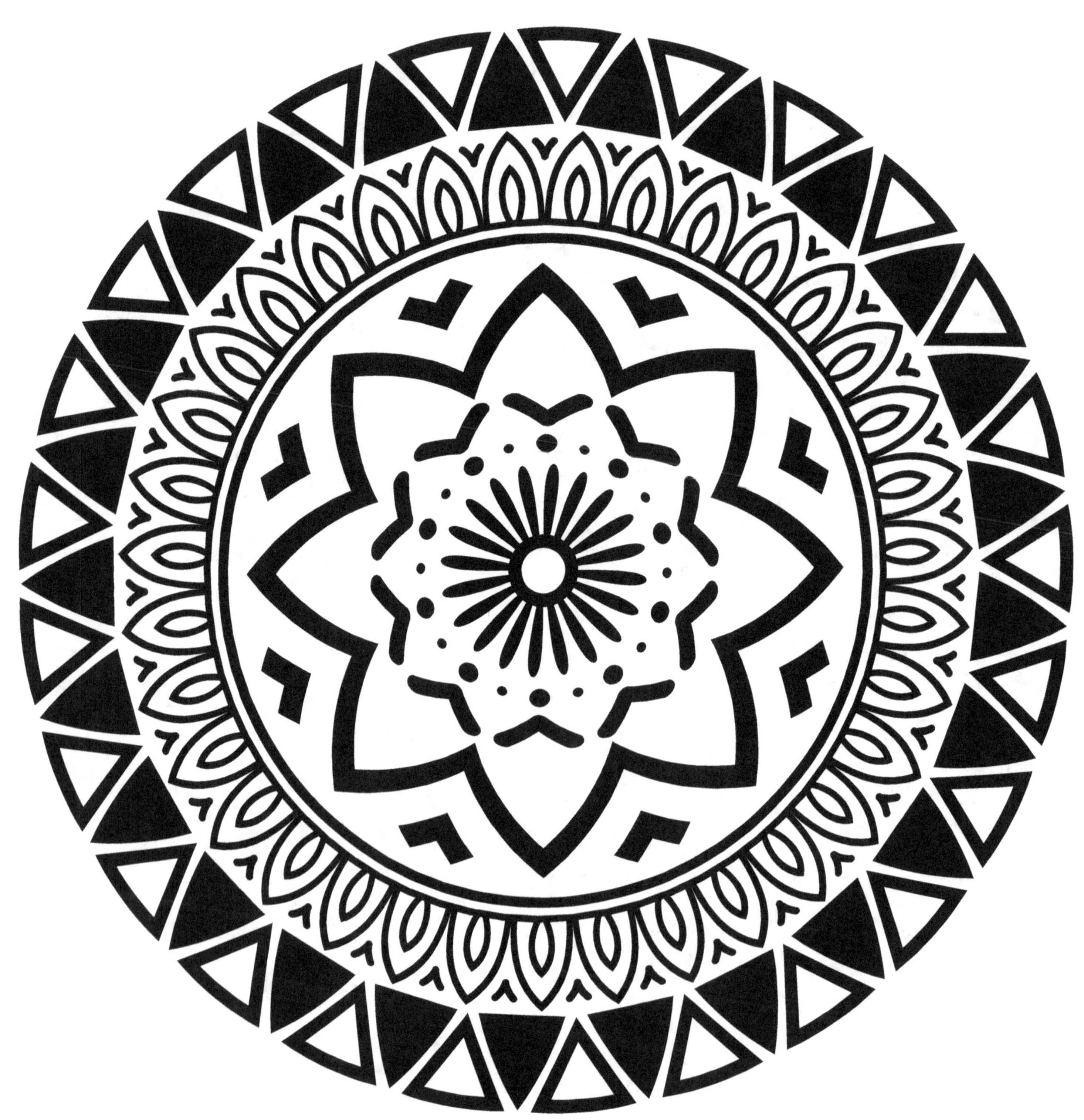

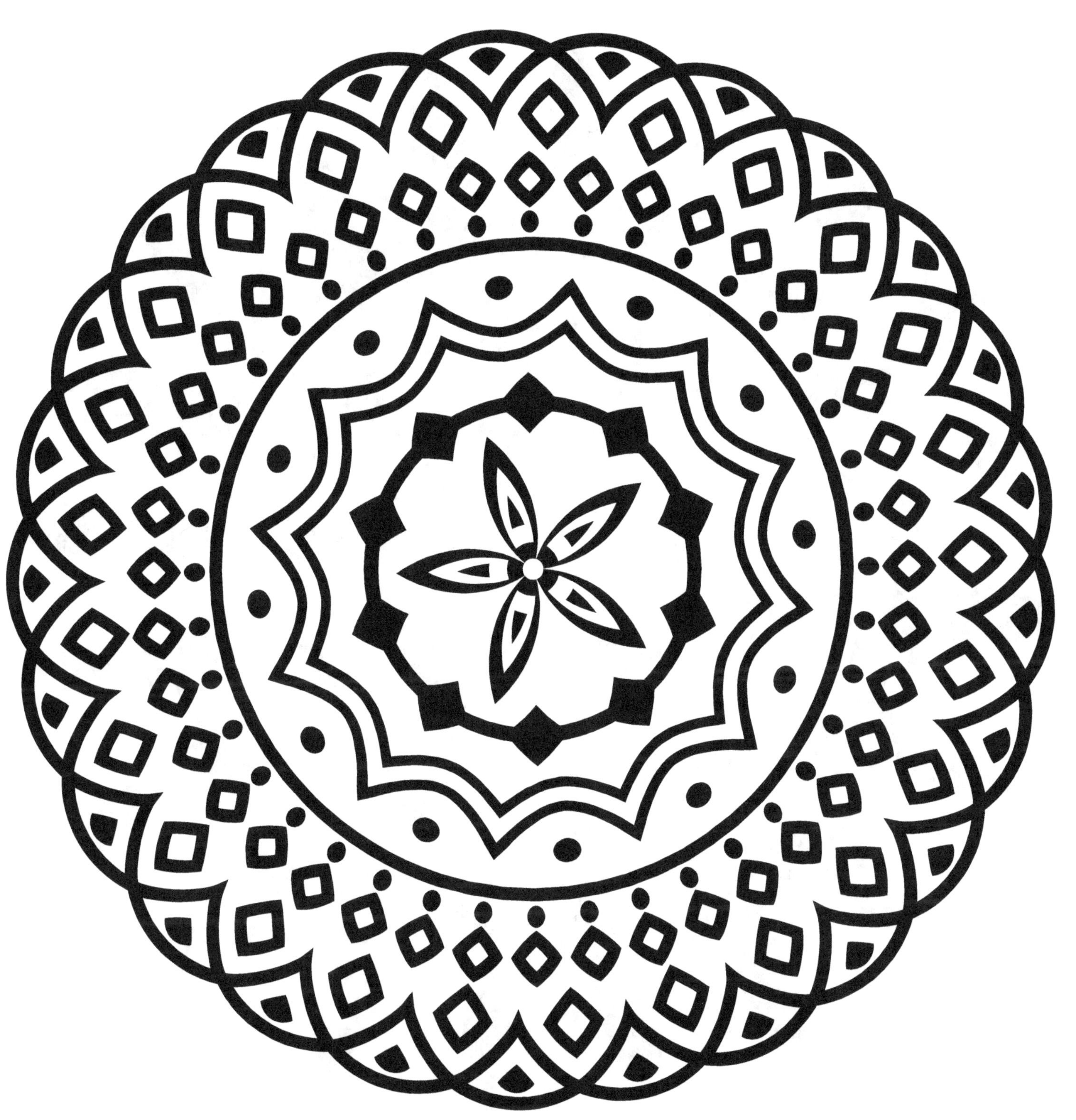

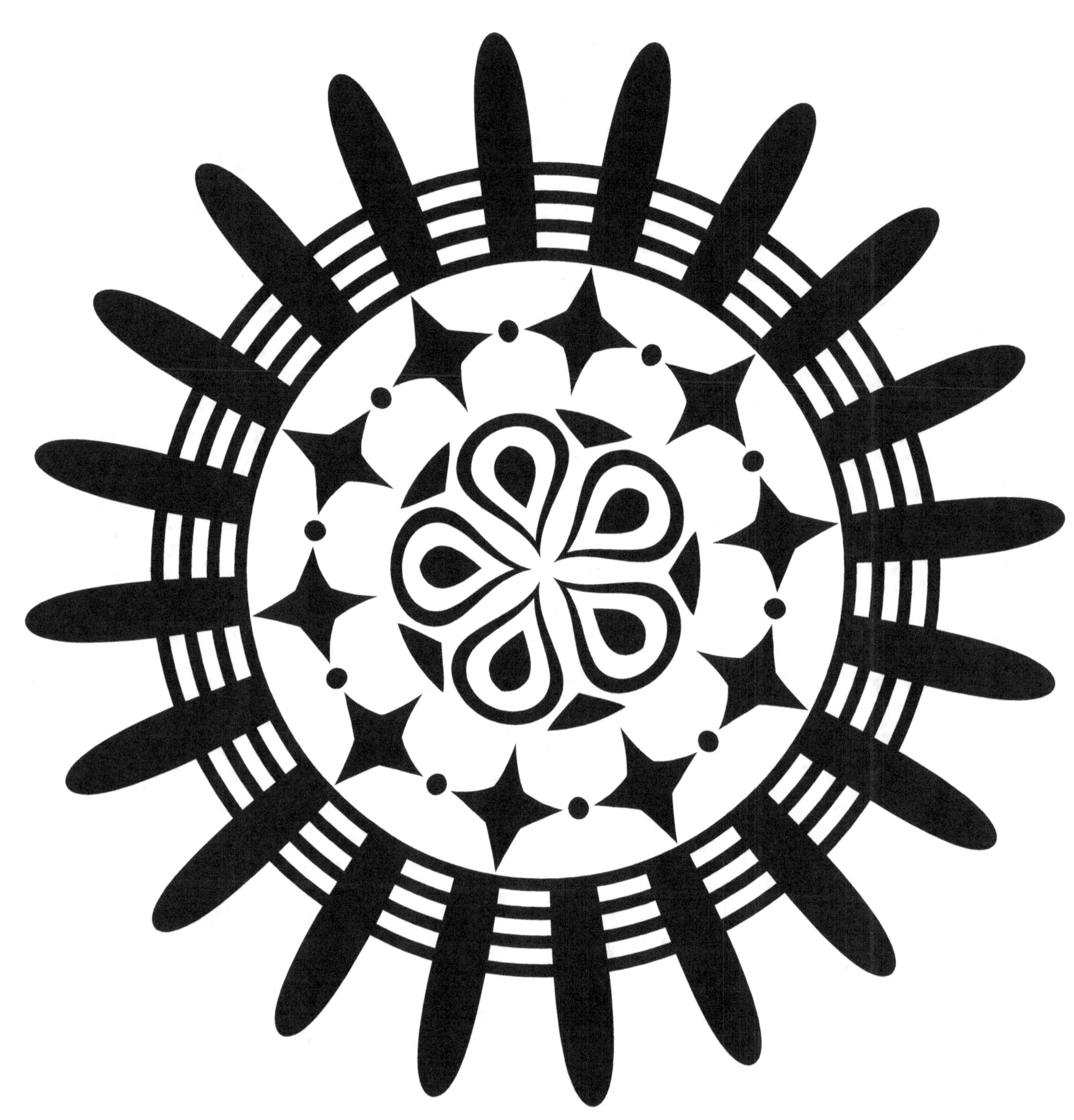

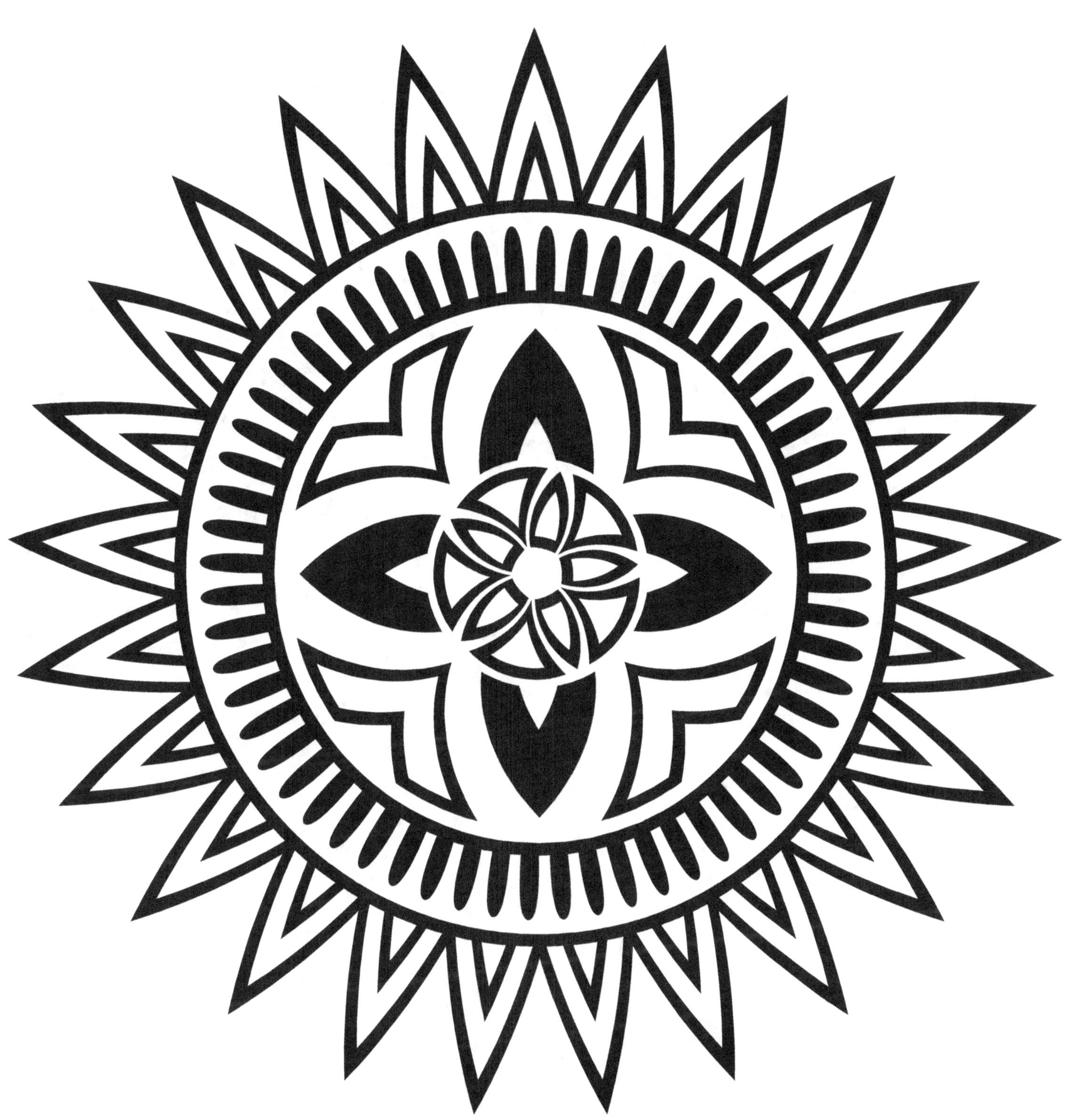

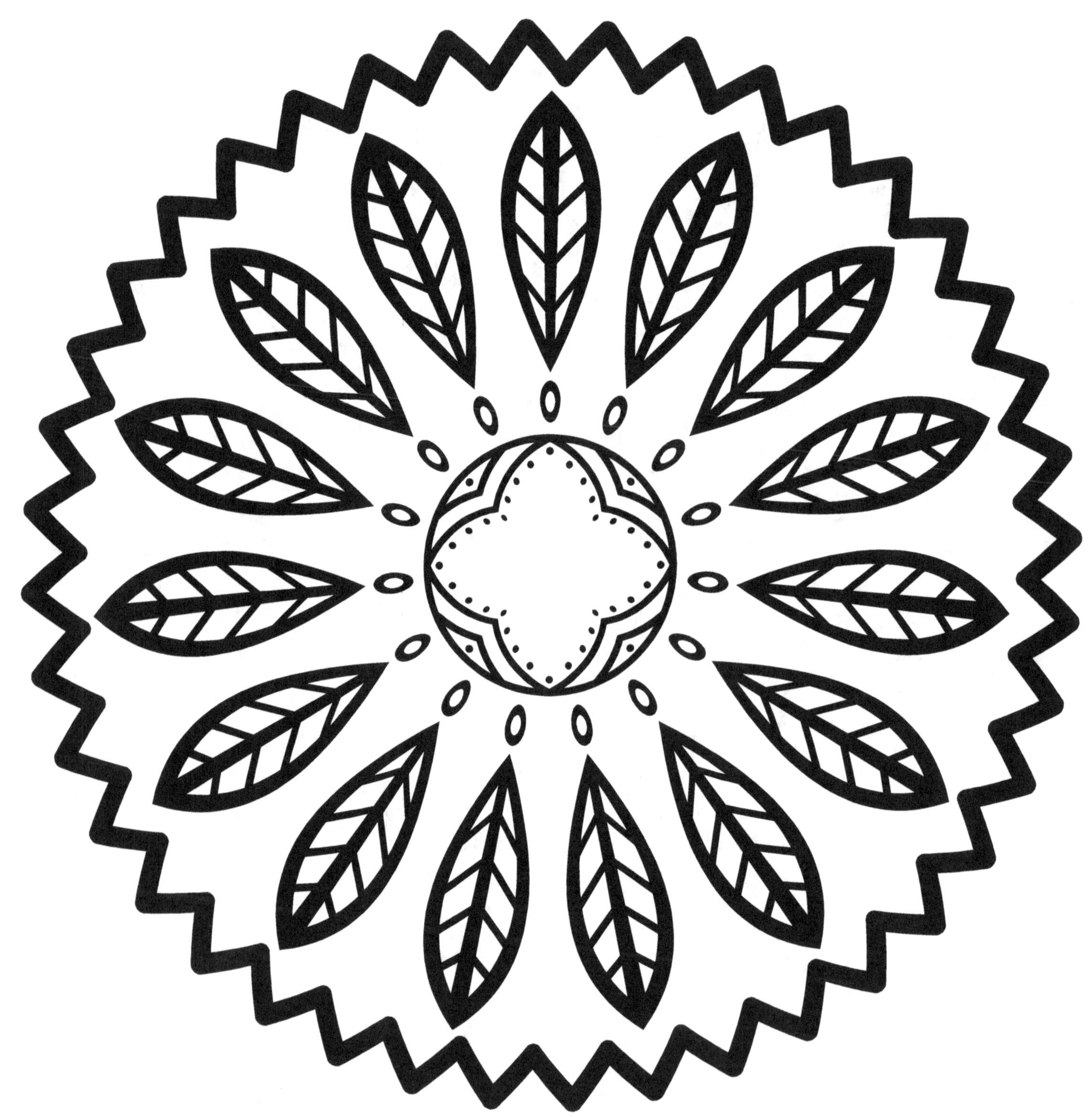

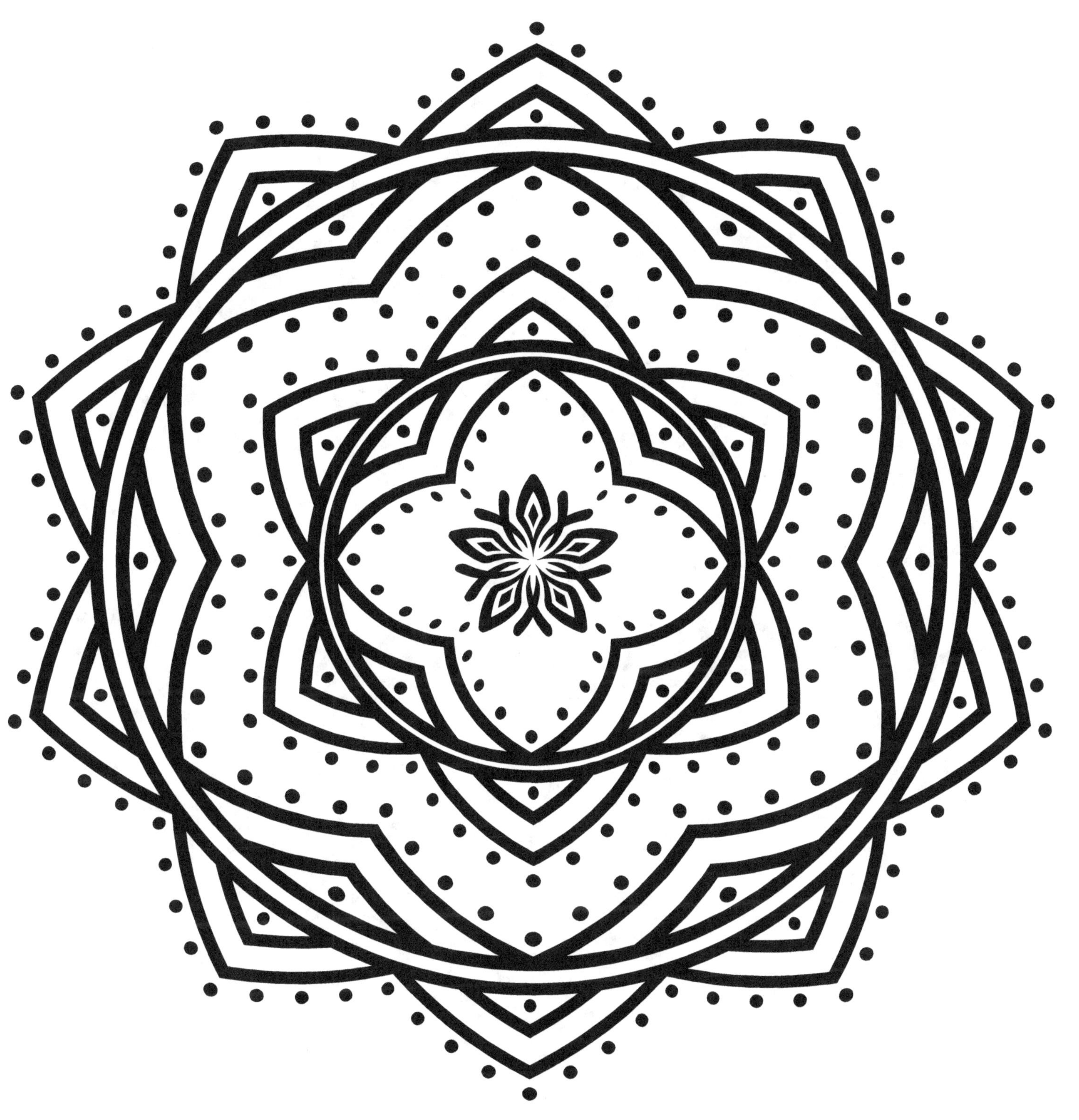

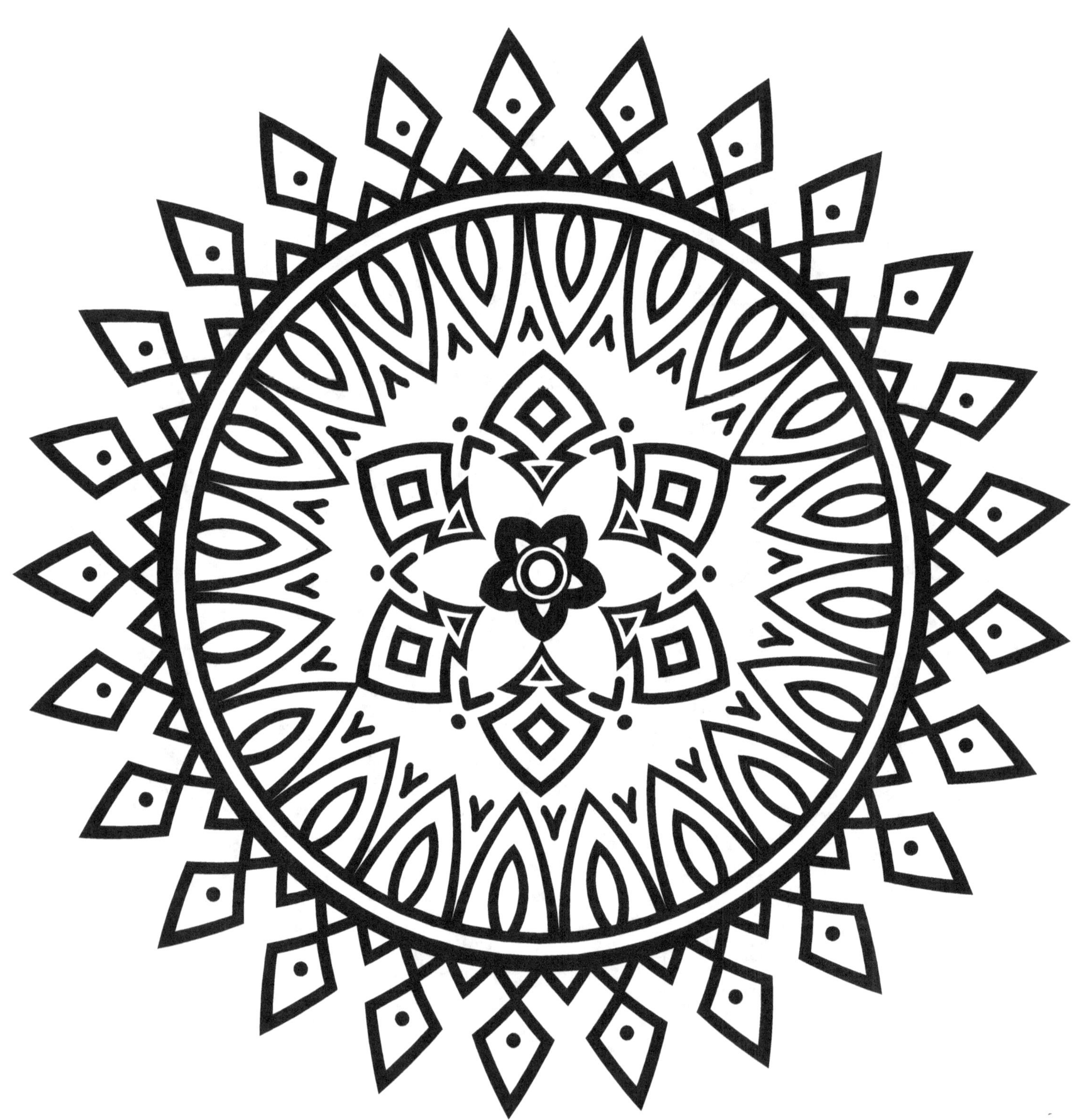